DELICIOUSLY VEGAN

90 tasty plant-based recipes for every occasion!

DELICIOUSLY VEGAN

THE CHIC NATURAL

Contents

Introduction · 1

BREAKFAST & BRUNCH · 3

Cinnamon Vanilla French Toast 5 · Glazed Apple Cinnamon Breakfast Donuts 6 · Chik'n & Waffles 8 · Good Morning Granola Cereal 9 · Sweet French Crêpes 11 · Spinach & Bell Pepper Tofu Scramble 13 · Pumpkin Spice Pancakes 14 · Buttermilk Cornbread Muffins 16 · Country Style Breakfast Potatoes 17 · Peach Almond Strudel 20 · Southern Style Veggies & Grits 21 · Fried Green Tomatoes Over Cheesy Grits 23 · Chickpea & Veggie Quiche Cups 24 · Chocolate Peanut Butter Breakfast Shake 25 · Very Vanilla Fruit Salad 25 · Cinnamon Crunch Banana Bread 27

APPETIZERS & SNACKS · 29

Vegetable Birds' Nests 31 · Better Than Refried Pinto Dip 32 · Green Bean Tempura w/ Sweet Soy Dipping Sauce 34 · Spinach & Artichoke Dip 36 · Buffalo Cauliflower Bites 37 · Herbed Dipping Oil 40 · Ginger Soy Glazed Edamame 41 · Coconut Crusted Shiitake Poppers 44 · Spicy Potato & Pea Fritters 45 · Summer Nori Rolls w/ Peanut Dipping Sauce 46 · Chickpea & Sun Dried Tomato Bruschetta w/ Balsamic Glaze 47

SOUPS & STEWS · 49

10 Minute Black Bean Soup 51 · Wild Rice & Mushroom Soup 52 · Cajun Corn & Quinoa Chowder 53 · Cheesy Broccoli & Potato Soup 56 · Roasted Garlic & Asparagus Soup 57 · West African Peanut Stew 58 · Coconut Curry Soup 59 · Cream of Zucchini Soup 62 · Cabbage & White Bean Soup 63 · Roasted Tomato Basil Soup 64 · Hearty Lentil Stew 66

SANDWICHES & WRAPS • 67

Lentil Meatball Marinara Sub 69 · Mushroom BLTA Sandwich 70 · Black Bean & Lentil BBQ Burgers 71 · Saucy Quinoa Veggie Wrap 73 · Tempeh Sloppy Joe Sandwiches 74 · Oyster Mushroom Po' Boy w/ Dill Remoulade Sauce 76 · Bang Bang Cauliflower Sandwich 77 · Spinach Mushroom Hummus Quesadillas 78 · Chickpea Salad Sandwich 79 · Chipotle Portobello Sheet Pan Fajitas 81 · Crispy Falafel Pita Wraps 82 · Blackened Tofu Caesar Wraps 83

SIDE DISHES • 85

Old Bay Potato Wedges w/ Smoked Buffalo Dipping Sauce 87 · Pan Steamed Garlic Kale 88 · Stir Fried Broccoli & Shiitake Mushrooms 90 · Cheesy Spinach Rice 91 · Old Fashioned Potato Salad 92 · Roasted Brussels Sprouts w/ Agave Mustard Glaze 93 · Mexican Street Corn Salad 95 · Balsamic Roasted Tahini Carrots 96 · Cheesy Stovetop Macaroni 97 · Herbed Garlic Smashed Red Potatoes 99 · Easy Summertime Slaw 101 · Kung Pao Cabbage 102 · Garden Pasta Salad 103

MAIN DISHES • 105

Kickin' Cajun Pasta w/ Sun Dried Tomatoes 107 · Roasted Red Pepper & Broccoli Fettuccini Alfredo 108 · Southwestern Quinoa Stuffed Peppers 110 · Salisbury Lentil Steak 111 · Smokey Chickpea & Black Bean Meatloaf 112 · Pasta Primavera Bake 113 · Herbed Vegetable Pot Pies 115 · General Tso's Cauliflower 117 · Crispy Tofu Stir Fry 119 · One Pot Mushroom Stroganoff 120 · Margherita Pizza 121 · Maryland Style Crab-Less Cakes 124 · Cauliflower Parmesan Bake 125 · Black Bean Lasagna 127

DESSERTS · 128

Iced Lemon Loaf Cake 130 · Classic Apple Pie 131 · Oatmeal Raisin Cookies 132 · The Best Peanut Butter Cookies 133 · Lemon Blueberry Muffins 136 · 1 Hour Cinnamon Rolls 137 · Strawberry Cheesecake Minis 140 · Soft Baked Gingersnap Cookies 141 · Blueberry Twist Bread 143 · Raspberry Almond Thumbprint Cookies 145 · Double Chocolate Cake w/ Buttercream Frosting 146 · Candy Bar Shortbread Cookies 148 · Chewy Snickerdoodle Cookies 149

Acknowledgements · 151

Conversion Charts · 153

Introduction

I'm going to tell a secret that may be surprising to some of you. Before going plant-based I couldn't cook. No joke, I was terrible at it. Growing up my "skills" in the kitchen were non-existent at best and looking back it always gives me a good chuckle at just how bad I was. I would spend hours on dishes that I saw on some television show or try to recreate something I ate at a restaurant, or heck, even something simple like spaghetti, and it would most times turn out inedible. My family would gather around the stove to make jokes about my latest attempt. It was a thing.

After a while I pretty much stopped trying and stuck to the very basics while mostly filling up on fast food and convenience meals from the supermarket. I shudder thinking of the days where home cooked meals were a rarity for me. But several years ago I decided I needed a change and made the decision to go completely plant-based and my entire world was turned upside down…in a way I didn't see happening.

You see, all of my family and friends are meat eaters. Cooking meals without animal products isn't something they knew much about so I couldn't rely on someone else's food to sustain me. There was no vegan fast food. Also at the time vegan cuisine at the supermarket wasn't as accessible or plentiful as it is now and my vegan options at restaurants were few and far between when we would go out to eat. That meant one thing: I needed to learn how to cook once and for all if I was going to stick with this new way of eating.

I got back in the kitchen with a determination to make food that was actually tasty and filling. I made it a point to go in with an open mind. If I was going to make this work then I had to be open to trying new things and abandoning my previous picky food biases. This turned out to be the magic key. It was as if a whole new world opened up to me.

I started out by "vegan-izing" foods that I already liked to eat and went from there. In the beginning there were definitely some hiccups, but as time went on it became easier and easier to navigate my way around the kitchen. I started surprising myself at how much I not only enjoyed cooking but how I could create new flavors I had never tasted, simply by experimenting and mixing things together.

During my dietary transition I started posting videos documenting what I ate which began to become extremely well received so I kept going and kept sharing. I realized I had a real knack and love for cooking and it would bring me so much joy and pride each time I came up with another winning dish.

Cooking is such a communal activity and it definitely brings you closer to your loved ones as well. Bringing my kids into the kitchen with me to show them how to make this or that, explaining the ingredients and the processes, is such a bonding experience. Not to mention the fact that I can now give my family home cooked food that I am proud of, food that is packed with fruits, vegetables, beans and grains. Food made with love. This journey and my renewed interest in all things culinary has enriched all of our lives in so many ways.

I love bringing my meat-eating family and friends into my plant-based world and seeing how intrigued and excited they get when I let them try my new creations. To know that these dishes can satisfy all palates is the true measure of success to me.

This cookbook is my literal culinary Cinderella story and I hope it shows you the ease, simplicity and deliciousness of vegan foods. Within these pages you will find a culmination of my tried-and-true recipes over the years. Recipes that have brought not only myself, but the people around me a lot of happiness…and now I'm sharing them with all of you.

No matter where you are in your journey, whether you're just starting out and making your first dish or simply looking to shake things up and find your next vegan go-to, my aim is that this book inspires you along the way.

From my kitchen to yours,

-The Chic Natural

Breakfast & Brunch

Cinnamon Vanilla French Toast

PREP TIME: 5 minutes • **COOK TIME:** 10 minutes • **MAKES:** 4 slices

An indulgent dish perfect for breakfast or a weekend brunch. Classic and easy to whip up, this french toast is filled with notes of cinnamon and vanilla.

- 4 slices sourdough bread
- ½ cup almond milk
- ½ teaspoon vanilla extract
- 1 teaspoon nutritional yeast
- 2 teaspoons flour
- 1 teaspoon cinnamon
- ⅛ teaspoon nutmeg
- 1 teaspoon sugar

In a large shallow bowl whisk almond milk, vanilla extract, nutritional yeast, flour, cinnamon and sugar until thoroughly mixed.

Preheat greased griddle to medium heat.

Dip each piece of bread in the batter so that both sides are well coated, then place on griddle. Cook until golden brown on the underside, gently pressing down a few times on the middle of the bread with a spatula to ensure it is evenly heated.

Carefully flip and cook for another 3-4 minutes until the other side is golden brown as well.

Glazed Apple Cinnamon Breakfast Donuts

PREP TIME: 5 minutes • **COOK TIME:** 10 minutes • **MAKES:** 6 donuts

Light and fluffy, filled with tart granny smith apples and sweet cinnamon sugar these easy baked donuts are a true breakfast treat!

- 3 tablespoons vegan butter, melted
- 3 tablespoons vegetable oil
- ¼ cup sugar
- 1 tablespoon applesauce
- 1 teaspoon vanilla extract
- ½ cup almond milk
- 1 ⅓ cup flour
- 1 teaspoon cinnamon
- ½ tablespoon baking powder
- ⅛ teaspoon baking soda
- ⅛ teaspoon salt
- 1 granny smith apple, finely chopped
- 2 tablespoons pecans, chopped

GLAZE
- ½ cup powdered sugar
- ⅛ teaspoon cinnamon
- 1 teaspoon maple syrup
- 2 teaspoons almond milk

Preheat oven to 425 degrees F.

In a large mixing bowl combine melted butter, oil, sugar, applesauce, vanilla extract and almond milk then whisk until smooth.

Next, mix in flour, cinnamon, baking powder, baking soda, salt and chopped apples until fully combined.

Using a cookie scoop or piping bag pipe batter into lightly greased donut molds and bake for 10 minutes. They will be golden brown and set.

Allow donuts to cool for 10 minutes.

In a small bowl whisk together the ingredients for the glaze. Dip each donut into the glaze and place on a plate or wire rack.

Sprinkle on chopped pecans if desired (optional).

Chik'n & Waffles

PREP TIME: 10 minutes • **COOK TIME:** 10 minutes • **MAKES:** 2 servings

This decadent dish of soft, fluffy waffles topped with juicy fried seasoned mushrooms is the ultimate sweet and savory breakfast or brunch!

PORTOBELLO "CHIK'N"
2 portobello mushroom caps, each cut into thirds
vegetable oil for frying

WET BATTER:
¼ cup flour
½ teaspoon cajun seasoning
¼ teaspoon onion powder
¼ teaspoon garlic powder
⅛ teaspoon cumin
½ cup almond milk

DRY BATTER:
⅓ cup flour
¼ cup breadcrumbs
¼ teaspoon salt
⅛ teaspoon pepper

WAFFLES
1 cup flour
1 cup almond milk
¼ cup applesauce
1 teaspoon coconut oil, melted
½ teaspoon vanilla extract
2 teaspoons brown sugar
¼ teaspoon baking soda
⅛ teaspoon salt

Prepare the batters for the sliced mushroom caps. First, in a medium bowl add the wet ingredients and stir to fully combine. In a separate medium bowl add the dry ingredients and whisk together.

Add about 3/4" of vegetable oil to a skillet and heat over medium heat.

While the oil is warming, prepare the waffle batter by combining flour, almond milk, applesauce, melted coconut oil, vanilla extract, brown sugar and baking soda in a bowl. Pour into a seasoned waffle iron once it's heated up. Cook for 5 minutes.

When the oil in the skillet starts to sizzle, dredge each mushroom piece fully into the wet batter, then transfer to the dry batter to coat. Add each breaded mushroom piece to the skillet and fry for about 3 minutes until the underside becomes golden brown. Flip and fry an additional 2-3 minutes until crispy throughout. Remove from oil and place on paper towels to drain excess oil.

Place cooked waffle on a plate and top with 3 fried mushroom pieces each. Drizzle with maple syrup and/or hot sauce if desired.

Good Morning Granola Cereal

PREP TIME: 5 minutes • **COOK TIME:** 20 minutes • **MAKES:** 5-6 servings

This crunchy mix of spiced oats, raisins, almonds and coconut lightly sweetened with maple syrup makes for the perfect cereal. It's also great as a topping on ice cream, yogurt and more!

2 cups rolled oats
½ cup sliced almonds
¼ cup ground flax seeds
2 tablespoons vegan butter, melted
½ teaspoon vanilla extract
⅓ cup maple syrup
1 ½ teaspoon cinnamon
¼ teaspoon nutmeg
½ cup unsweetened coconut flakes
½ cup raisins

Preheat oven to 350 degrees F.

In a large bowl combine oats, almonds and ground flax seeds.

In a separate bowl whisk together melted vegan butter, vanilla extract, maple syrup, cinnamon and nutmeg. Pour over oat mixture and stir to fully combine.

Press granola into a single layer on a lined baking sheet. Bake for 10 minutes, stirring half way. Remove from oven, mix in coconut flakes and raisins, and bake an additional 8-10 minutes until golden brown and crisp throughout. Let cool before removing from baking sheet.

Sweet French Crepes

PREP TIME: 5 minutes • **COOK TIME:** 5 minutes • **MAKES:** 5 crepes

So fancy, yet so simple! Make perfect crepes in minutes with only 7 ingredients! Fill with whatever you like- sweet or savory. These are super versatile!

½ cup flour
¾ cup almond milk
2 tablespoons applesauce
½ tablespoon coconut oil, melted
¼ tablespoon vanilla extract
1 teaspoon brown sugar
⅛ teaspoon salt

Place all ingredients into a mixing bowl whisk until batter is smooth with no lumps left.

Lightly grease a large skillet and place over medium heat. Once the pan is heated, scoop about ¼ cup of batter into the pan, then quickly swirl so the batter evenly spreads out into a thin circle.

Cook for about 2 minutes until the edges of the crepe turn brown and the top starts to appear dry, then carefully flip the crepe with a spatula and cook for another minute or two.

Flip the crepe once more and cook for an additional 30 seconds to ensure its cooked through.

Serve the crepes rolled up with any fillings or toppings you like. Fresh fruit inside and a drizzle of chocolate syrup on top pair amazingly well!

Spinach & Bell Pepper Tofu Scramble

PREP TIME: 5 minutes • **COOK TIME:** 13 minutes • **MAKES:** 2 servings

Quick and easy this tasty scramble is a great way to start your day and will quickly become a staple in your breakfast repertoire!

8 oz tofu, extra firm
1 tablespoon olive oil
¼ red onion, diced
¼ red bell pepper, chopped
¼ green bell pepper, chopped
1 cup spinach, fresh
½ teaspoon turmeric
1 ½ teaspoon sea salt
1 teaspoon pepper

In a large skillet over medium-high heat sauté the onion and bell peppers in olive oil and cook until softened, about 5 minutes.

Drain tofu and press out excess liquid, then crumble and add to the pan. Cook for another 5 minutes until tofu is lightly browned.

Sprinkle turmeric over tofu and mix well, then add in spinach and cook about 2 minutes until spinach is wilted.

Mix in salt and pepper to taste and it's ready to serve!

Pumpkin Spice Pancakes

PREP TIME: 5 minutes • **COOK TIME:** 5 minutes • **MAKES:** 6-8 pancakes

Light and fluffy with just the right amount of pumpkin spice, these pancakes taste amazing topped with a little vegan butter and maple syrup!

1 cup flour
2 tablespoons sugar
1 tablespoon brown sugar
1 tablespoon baking powder
1 teaspoon pumpkin pie spice
½ teaspoon cinnamon
¼ teaspoon salt
¾ cup almond milk
¼ cup pureed pumpkin
2 tablespoons vegan butter, melted
1 tablespoon applesauce
1 tablespoon vegetable oil

In a large bowl stir together the flour, sugar, brown sugar, baking powder, pumpkin pie spice, cinnamon and salt.

Mix in the milk, pumpkin puree, vegan butter and applesauce and combine until a smooth batter forms.

Heat a skillet over medium heat. Add vegetable oil to coat the bottom of the pan and once it starts to sizzle pour in about ¼ cup of the batter.

Cook 3-4 minutes until the top of the pancake starts to bubble and the underside becomes golden brown.

Flip and cook for another minute or 2 until the other side is golden brown.

Buttermilk Cornbread Muffins

PREP TIME: 5 minutes • **COOK TIME:** 30 minutes • **MAKES:** 8 muffins

Moist and buttery cornbread muffins are tasty enough to stand on their own as a quick breakfast or use for a simple side dish or snack!

¾ cup almond milk
1 teaspoon apple cider vinegar
1 cup flour
¾ cup cornmeal
⅓ cup sugar
1 tablespoon baking powder
½ teaspoon salt
1 tablespoon applesauce
¼ cup vegan butter, melted

Preheat oven to 350 degrees F and line a muffin pan with 8 paper liners.

Prepare vegan buttermilk by whisking together almond milk and apple cider vinegar in a small bowl. Let sit for about 5 minutes until the milk starts to curdle.

Add flour, cornmeal, sugar, baking powder and salt to a large bowl and combine thoroughly.

Pour the buttermilk into the dry bowl, then add applesauce and melted vegan butter. Mix well until you get a smooth batter.

Fill muffin tins ¾ full with batter. Bake for 25-30 minutes until set and the tops are a light golden brown.

Country Style Breakfast Potatoes

PREP TIME: 7 minutes • **COOK TIME:** 25 minutes • **MAKES:** 2-3 servings

Crispy on the outside and tender on the inside, these potatoes are made with simple ingredients and wonderfully seasoned!

- 3 large russet potatoes
- ¼ red bell pepper
- ¼ green bell pepper
- ¼ cup red onion, diced
- 1 tablespoon fresh rosemary, finely chopped
- 2 tablespoons olive oil
- ½ teaspoon salt
- ¼ teaspoon pepper
- ½ tablespoon seasoned salt
- 1 ½ tablespoons maple syrup

Cut washed potatoes into cubes. Add cubed potatoes to a pot and fill with enough water to cover them, then bring to a rolling boil and cook for about 7 minutes until tender and easily pierced with a fork. Drain and set potatoes aside.

Meanwhile, dice the bell peppers and red onion and chop the rosemary.

In a large skillet over medium heat add 1 tablespoon of olive oil and the potatoes and cook for 10 minutes until potatoes have started to brown, stirring often in order to brown evenly.

Drizzle remaining 1 tablespoon of olive oil into the skillet, then add bell peppers, onion and rosemary and cook an additional 5 minutes until peppers are tender and onions translucent, again stirring often.

Season with salt, pepper and season salt then mix well.

Remove from heat. Drizzle maple syrup over potatoes and toss, then serve hot.

Peach Almond Strudel

PREP TIME: 10 minutes • **COOK TIME:** 25 minutes • **MAKES:** 6 servings

A peach and sweet vegan cream cheese filling wrapped in puff pastry, topped with almonds, and baked to a golden perfection! This strudel makes for a lovely breakfast or enjoy for dessert!

FILLING
2 tablespoons vegan butter
1 teaspoon flour
1 tablespoon sugar
2 ½ tablespoons brown sugar, divided
1 tablespoon water
1 peach, peeled and diced
3 tablespoons vegan cream cheese
½ teaspoon vanilla extract

1 sheet vegan-friendly puff pastry, thawed
2 teaspoons vegan butter, melted
1 tablespoon sliced almonds
powdered sugar

Preheat oven to 400 degrees F and lightly grease or line a baking sheet with parchment paper.

Prepare the filling by adding vegan butter to a pan over medium heat. Once melted, add flour and whisk to form a paste. Pour in sugar, 1 tablespoon of brown sugar, and water and stir about 2-3 minutes until the mixture resembles a thick syrup. Add in diced peaches and toss to coat. Remove from heat and set aside.

Next, in a small bowl mix together vegan cream cheese, 1 ½ tablespoons of brown sugar and vanilla extract.

Unfold puff pastry onto the baking sheet- you will have 3 rectangular sections. Make five diagonal cuts about 1 ½" apart from each other on the outer 2 sections. Spread cream cheese mixture evenly onto the center section of the puff pastry. Top with the coated peaches.

Fold over the side strips of the pastry toward the middle section in a criss-cross fashion to cover the filling. Brush the top of the pastry with 1 teaspoon of melted vegan butter, then bake for 10 minutes.

Remove from oven, brush with remaining melted butter and sprinkle the top with almonds. Bake an additional 10-12 minutes until the pasty is fluffy and lightly browned. Finish with a dusting of powdered sugar.

Southern Style Veggies & Grits

PREP TIME: 10 minutes • **COOK TIME:** 15 minutes • **MAKES:** 4 servings

Cajun seasoned spinach and mushrooms over a bed of rich cheesy grits, it's delicious comfort food at its best.

CHEESY GRITS
1 ¼ cup grits, quick-cooking
1 ½ cups water
1 cup vegetable broth
1 cup almond milk
¼ cup nutritional yeast
1 teaspoon salt
3 tablespoons vegan butter

SPINACH MUSHROOM TOPPING
1 tablespoon olive oil
1 cup mushrooms, sliced
2 cups spinach
1 teaspoon garlic powder
½ teaspoon cajun seasoning

Prepare grits by mixing together water, vegetable broth, almond milk, nutritional yeast and salt. Place in a pot over medium-high heat and bring to a boil.

Slowly whisk in the grits to prevent clumping, then reduce heat to low. Cover and cook 12-14 minutes or until thickened, stirring occasionally. When most of the liquid is absorbed stir in the vegan butter.

While the grits are cooking prepare the spinach and mushroom topping by first placing olive oil in a large skillet over medium heat. Once the oil starts to sizzle add sliced mushrooms and spinach and sauté for about 5 minutes until vegetables are tender. Sprinkle in garlic powder and cajun seasoning then toss to fully coat.

Place grits in bowls and equally top with spinach and mushrooms.

Fried Green Tomatoes over Cheesy Grits

PREP TIME: 10 minutes • **COOK TIME:** 15 minutes • **MAKES:** 4 servings

Fried green tomatoes are crisp and golden brown on the outside, tangy and tender on the inside. Served over dairy-free cheesy grits, it's a savory Southern favorite turned vegan.

CHEESY GRITS
- 1 ¼ cup grits, quick-cooking
- 1 ½ cups water
- 1 cup vegetable broth
- 1 cup almond milk
- ¼ cup nutritional yeast
- 1 teaspoon salt
- 3 tablespoons vegan butter

FRIED GREEN TOMATOES
- 2 large green tomatoes
- ½ cup cornstarch
- ½ cup vegan mayonnaise
- ¼ cup almond milk
- 1 ½ cup breadcrumbs
- 1 ½ teaspoons onion powder
- 1 ½ teaspoons garlic powder
- 1 ½ teaspoons oregano
- 1 teaspoon salt
- 1 cup vegetable oil

Prepare grits as on page 21.

While the grits are cooking, place cornstarch in a shallow bowl. In another shallow bowl whisk together vegan mayonnaise and almond milk. In a third bowl combine breadcrumbs, onion powder, garlic powder, oregano and salt.

Chop off the ends of the tomatoes and cut each into 4 round slices.

Dredge each tomato slice first in the cornstarch. Shake off any excess, then dip them in the mayonnaise mixture. Now dredge tomato slices in the breadcrumb mixture.

In a skillet heat the oil until bubbling. Place the battered tomatoes in the oil and fry 2-3 minutes on each side. Drain excess oil on paper towels.

Serve fried tomatoes over grits.

Chickpea & Veggie Quiche Cups

PREP TIME: 5 minutes • **COOK TIME:** 40 minutes • **MAKES:** 6 quiche cups

These bite-sized baked chickpea cups are an easy and portable breakfast! Load them up with your favorite veggies for the best meal on the go!

1 cup chickpea flour
½ cup almond milk
¼ cup water
1 teaspoon mustard
3 teaspoons nutritional yeast
¼ teaspoon baking powder
½ teaspoon garlic powder
½ teaspoon onion powder
½ teaspoon salt
⅛ teaspoon pepper
1 ½ tablespoon olive oil
⅓ cup corn kernels
⅓ cup red bell pepper, diced
¼ cup zucchini, diced
¼ cup red onion, diced
⅓ cup spinach, chopped
1 scallion, chopped

Preheat oven to 425 degrees F. Grease or spray 6 cups of a standard size muffin tin.

In a large bowl whisk together the chickpea flour, almond milk, water, mustard, nutritional yeast, baking powder and seasonings until blended and smooth.

In a skillet heat the olive oil over medium-high heat then add corn, bell pepper, zucchini and red onion. Cook about 5 minutes until vegetables are softened and start to brown.

Add spinach and scallions and cook an additional 2 minutes, stirring frequently.

Transfer the vegetables to the chickpea batter and mix until well combined.

Fill the muffin tins with the batter just below the top, then bake for 25-30 minutes until a toothpick comes out clean when inserted into the center. The omelet cups will be puffed slightly and golden brown.

Let cool at least 5 minutes before removing from muffin sheet.

Chocolate Peanut Butter Breakfast Shake

PREP TIME: 5 minutes • **MAKES:** 1 large shake

This morning milkshake is loaded with so many good things: protein rich peanut butter, sweet and natural coconut sugar, almond milk, and notes of cocoa and vanilla. It's a thick and creamy healthy breakfast treat!

1 medium banana
¼ cup peanut butter
1 teaspoon cacao powder
1 tablespoon coconut sugar
½ teaspoon vanilla extract
1 cup almond milk
6 ice cubes

Place all ingredients into a blender and pulse until completely smooth.

Pour into a glass and enjoy cold.

Very Vanilla Fruit Salad

PREP TIME: 10 minutes • **REFRIGERATE:** 1 hour • **MAKES:** 3-4 servings

Simple, fresh and delicious! Can be easily customized to include your favorite fruits!

1 kiwi
½ cup blueberries
½ cup pineapple
1 cup strawberries
½ cup cantaloupe
2 tablespoons powdered sugar
1 teaspoon vanilla extract

Dice kiwi, pineapple, strawberries and cantaloupe. Place into a large bowl along with blueberries, powdered sugar and vanilla extract.

Mix thoroughly to combine.

Cover and refrigerate for 1 hour or until ready to serve.

Cinnamon Crunch Banana Bread

PREP TIME: 10 minutes • **COOK TIME:** 60 minutes • **MAKES:** 10 slices

Packed with mashed bananas this whole wheat breakfast delight comes together quickly and easily in one bowl!

- 2 medium bananas, mashed
- ¼ cup applesauce
- ½ cup plain vegan yogurt
- ⅓ cup vegetable oil
- 1 ¾ cups whole wheat flour
- ½ cup sugar
- ¼ cup cornstarch
- 1 ½ teaspoons baking powder
- 2 teaspoons cinnamon
- ¼ teaspoon salt

CINNAMON CRUNCH TOPPING
- ¼ cup flour
- ¼ cup brown sugar
- ½ teaspoon cinnamon
- 2 tablespoons vegan butter, cold

Preheat oven to 375 degrees F and line an 8" loaf pan with parchment paper.

Whisk together mashed bananas, applesauce, vegan yogurt, and vegetable oil in a large bowl. Add flour, sugar, cornstarch, baking powder, cinnamon and salt and mix until just combined.

In a separate bowl prepare the topping by adding flour, brown sugar and cinnamon and mixing well. Add cold vegan butter and with your hands knead and work it in until the mixture is thoroughly combined and turns crumbly.

Transfer batter to loaf pan, then evenly sprinkle with cinnamon crunch topping.

Bake for 55-60 minutes until firm and an inserted toothpick comes out clean. Let cool at least 10 minutes before removing from pan.

Appetizers & Snacks

Vegetable Birds' Nests

PREP TIME: 10 minutes • **COOK TIME:** 5 minutes • **MAKES:** 8-10

These birds' nests are spicy, light and addictively crispy. No one will be able to resist!

- 2 medium carrots, peeled
- ½ medium white onion
- ½ jalapeño pepper
- ¾ cup chickpea flour
- ½ teaspoon baking powder
- ½ teaspoon ground cumin
- ½ teaspoon turmeric
- 1 teaspoon salt
- ¼ cup water
- 1 teaspoon lemon juice
- 2 tablespoons fresh cilantro, chopped
- vegetable oil for frying

Spiralize the carrots then finely chop the onion and jalapeño pepper.

In a large bowl whisk together chickpea flour, baking powder, cumin, turmeric and salt. Pour in water and lemon juice and stir until a very thick batter forms.

Add the carrots, onion and jalapeño to the bowl along with cilantro and combine by kneading vegetables into the batter with your hands.

Heat ½" of vegetable oil in a skillet over medium high heat. Once hot, drop spoonfuls of the vegetable mixture into the oil at least ¾" apart.

Fry for 4-5 minutes until crispy and golden brown, flipping once.

Serve warm and eat as is or dip into soy sauce or vegan ranch dressing.

Better-Than-Refried Pinto Dip

PREP TIME: 5 minutes • **COOK TIME:** 20 minutes • **MAKES:** 4 servings

Who doesn't love a good dip?! This warm pinto bean dip comes together in just minutes and is a great party snack. You can also use it as a filling in burritos and tacos!

- 1 (15oz) can pinto beans, drained and rinsed
- ¼ cup vegetable broth
- 1 tablespoon olive oil
- 1 ½ teaspoons minced garlic
- ⅓ cup picante sauce
- 1 ½ tablespoons taco seasoning
- 1 teaspoon lemon juice
- 2 tablespoons vegan sour cream
- 2 scallions, chopped
- tortilla chips

Place the beans and vegetable broth into a blender and pulse until mostly smooth, but not liquified. Set aside.

Add olive oil and minced garlic to a large skillet over medium heat and sauté about 3 minutes until garlic starts to brown.

To the skillet add pinto bean mixture, picante sauce, taco seasoning, lemon juice and vegan sour cream, then mix well.

Reduce heat to low and simmer for 5 minutes, stirring occasionally.

Remove from heat. Garnish dip with chopped scallions and serve with tortilla chips.

Green Bean Tempura w/ Sweet Soy Dipping Sauce

PREP TIME: 5 minutes • **COOK TIME:** 4 minutes • **MAKES:** 2-3 servings

Ready in minutes and incredibly crispy and light, green beans are coated in a simple batter and shallow fried, then served with a savory-sweet dipping sauce. You can use this recipe for most any other vegetable as well!

1 pound fresh green beans, trimmed
½ cup ice cold water
3 teaspoons vegan mayonnaise
½ cup pastry flour
½ teaspoon paprika
½ teaspoon garlic powder
½ teaspoon salt
vegetable oil for frying

DIPPING SAUCE
¼ cup soy sauce
¼ cup sweet chili sauce

Prepare dipping sauce by whisking together soy sauce and sweet chili sauce. Set aside.

In a large bowl, form the batter by whisking together cold water and vegan mayonnaise until mostly smooth, then add in flour, paprika, garlic powder and salt and mix well.

Transfer the green beans to the bowl and toss to coat thoroughly with the batter.

Heat about ½" of vegetable oil in a large pan over medium-high heat. Once oil is hot, begin frying beans in batches. Carefully put the battered green beans into the hot oil one at a time making sure they don't stick together.

Fry for about 3-4 minutes until golden, then remove from pan and drain excess oil on paper towels.

Serve straight after frying with dipping sauce on the side.

Spinach & Artichoke Dip

PREP TIME: 5 minutes • **COOK TIME:** 20 minutes • **MAKES:** 2-3 servings

Deliciously rich and perfectly creamy, this savory dip full of spinach and artichoke is sure to be a crowd favorite!

- 1 ¼ cup cashews, raw
- 1 cup almond milk
- 1 tablespoon lime juice
- ½ teaspoon rice vinegar
- ½ teaspoon cayenne pepper
- 1 ½ teaspoon salt
- 1 tablespoon coconut oil
- 3 teaspoons minced garlic
- 10 oz frozen chopped spinach
- ¾ cup artichoke hearts, roughly chopped
- 1 teaspoon Italian seasoning
- 1 teaspoon Old Bay seasoning

Add cashews to a small saucepan, top with water and boil for 15 minutes to soften, then remove from heat and drain.

Place cashews in a blender along with almond milk, lime juice, rice vinegar, cayenne pepper and salt and blend until creamy. Set mixture aside.

In a large skillet add coconut oil, minced garlic and spinach and sauté for 5 minutes over medium heat.

Reduce heat to low and pour cashew cream into the skillet then add in chopped artichoke hearts and mix well.

Once mixture is heated throughout, sprinkle on Italian and Old Bay seasonings and fold into the dip. Remove from heat and enjoy with crackers, toasted bread or vegetables.

Buffalo Cauliflower Bites

PREP TIME: 10 minutes • **COOK TIME:** 25 minutes • **MAKES:** 2 servings

Tender and crispy, breaded cauliflower is baked then tossed in a buttered hot sauce. A vegan take on traditional hot wings, these are the ultimate party favorite without the guilt!

½ head of cauliflower
1 cup chickpea flour
1 tsp garlic powder
1 tsp onion powder
½ tsp salt
½ tsp pepper
¾ cup water
⅓ cup hot wing sauce
2 tbsp vegan butter, melted

Preheat oven to 425 degrees F and line a large baking sheet with parchment paper.

Chop and separate cauliflower into bite sized florets.

In a large bowl combine the chickpea flour, garlic powder, onion powder, salt and pepper, then slowly mix in the water until a thick batter is formed.

Add cauliflower pieces into the bowl and toss until well coated with the batter. Place on baking sheet and bake for about 20 minutes or until browned and crispy, turning halfway through.

While the cauliflower is in the oven mix together the hot wing sauce and melted butter in a large bowl.

Toss cooked cauliflower pieces with the sauce then place back onto the baking sheet and bake for an additional 5 minutes.

Herbed Dipping Oil

PREP TIME: 5 minutes • **MAKES:** 4 servings

Olive oil infused with a blend of dried herbs makes an easy and delicious dip for warm, crusty bread.

⅛ teaspoon sea salt
¼ teaspoon nutritional yeast
¼ teaspoon garlic powder
⅛ teaspoon red pepper flakes
⅛ teaspoon crushed rosemary
¼ cup extra virgin olive oil

Place salt, nutritional yeast flakes, garlic powder, red pepper flakes and rosemary in a small shallow dish. Mix to fully combine seasonings.

Pour olive oil over spices. Gently swirl dish to moisten.

Serve as a dipping sauce with crusty bread.

Ginger Soy Glazed Edamame

PREP TIME: 5 minutes • **COOK TIME:** 15 minutes • **MAKES:** 2 servings

Soybeans are upgraded to the next level in a finger licking sweetened ginger, soy, and garlic glaze.

- 2 cups frozen edamame, in pods
- 1 tablespoon sesame oil
- 1 tablespoon minced garlic
- 1 teaspoon minced ginger
- 2 tablespoons soy sauce
- 2 tablespoons maple syrup
- 1 teaspoon sriracha
- ¼ teaspoon red pepper flakes
- ¼ teaspoon salt

Place the edamame into a pot and add enough water to cover them, then boil for 8 minutes. Drain.

While the edamame is boiling add the soy sauce, maple syrup, sriracha and red chili flakes to a small bowl and whisk to combine.

Heat the sesame oil in a skillet over medium-low heat, then add minced garlic and ginger and cook 2 minutes, stirring frequently.

Add the drained edamame to the skillet and toss to coat with the oil mixture. Pour in the soy sauce mixture and stir well.

Turn up the heat to medium and mixing occasionally, cook for an additional 2-3 minutes until the sauce thickens and coats the edamame evenly.

Sprinkle with salt and serve warm.

Coconut Crusted Shiitake Poppers

PREP TIME: 10 minutes • **COOK TIME:** 20 minutes • **MAKES:** 2 servings

Amazingly easy to put together with a superb crunchy goodness, these shiitake poppers make for a great party appetizer or simply as a fun treat!

1 ½ cups shiitake mushrooms, sliced
¼ cup shredded coconut, unsweetened
⅓ cup Panko breadcrumbs
¼ cup spicy brown mustard
1 ½ tablespoons water
1 teaspoon maple syrup
¼ teaspoon salt
⅛ teaspoon pepper
olive oil

SPICY KETCHUP DIP
¼ cup ketchup
1 teaspoon hot sauce
½ teaspoon brown sugar

Preheat oven to 400 degrees F.

In a bowl combine coconut flakes and breadcrumbs.

In a separate bowl whisk together mustard, water, maple syrup, salt and pepper.

Take each shiitake slice and fully submerge into the mustard mixture.

Next, dip into the coconut mixture until completely coated and place on a lined baking sheet.

Spray tops of mushrooms with a light mist of olive oil.

Bake for 20 minutes until the mushrooms are cooked through and the outer coconut is light brown and toasted.

While mushrooms are in the oven prepare the spicy ketchup by mixing together ketchup, hot sauce and brown sugar. Serve as dip with shiitake poppers.

Spicy Potato & Pea Fritters

PREP TIME: 5 minutes • **COOK TIME:** 25 minutes • **MAKES:** 10-12 fritters

A beautifully spiced, flour coated snack deep fried to perfection!

2 medium potatoes, peeled and thinly sliced
½ cups peas
2 tablespoons cilantro, chopped
1 cup chickpea flour
1 teaspoon garam masala
¼ teaspoon chili powder
½ teaspoon cumin seeds
½ teaspoon salt
¼ cup water
vegetable oil for frying

Add potatoes, peas, cilantro, chickpea flour, garam masala, chili powder, cumin seeds and salt to a large bowl then mix well.

Slowly start to add warm water and mix in just until you achieve a thick batter that coats the vegetables and binds everything together.

Heat ¾" of oil in a deep frying pan over medium heat. Drop spoonfuls of the mixture into the oil and cook for about 5 minutes, flipping as needed to ensure even cooking.

Fry until both sides of the fritter are golden brown and crispy.

Drain on paper towels to absorb excess oil.

Enjoy plain or serve with a tangy chutney or ketchup.

Summer Nori Rolls w/ Peanut Dipping Sauce

PREP TIME: 20 minutes • **MAKES:** 10 rolls

Colorful and bright with the fresh taste of summer, these raw vegetable nori rolls accompanied with a spicy peanut dipping sauce are happiness in every bite!

2 sheets raw nori
2 tablespoons tahini
½ red bell pepper, sliced thin
½ yellow bell pepper, sliced thin
1 avocado, sliced
½ cup carrots, shredded
½ cup spring mix greens
salt and pepper

_____

SPICY PEANUT SAUCE
¼ cup creamy peanut butter
¼ cup water
½ teaspoon apple cider vinegar
½ teaspoon hot sauce
1 tablespoon maple syrup
¼ teaspoon red pepper flakes
¼ teaspoon ground ginger
¼ teaspoon salt
⅛ teaspoon pepper

Place ingredients for the spicy peanut sauce into a large bowl and whisk together until smooth and creamy. Set aside.

Lay out one sheet of nori with the long edge close to you. Spread one tablespoon of tahini thinly over the nori sheet.

Layer half of the bell peppers, carrots, avocado and greens on the bottom half of the sheet. Sprinkle with a pinch of salt and pepper.

Gently but firmly, roll the edge closest to you toward the center of the nori wrap into a sushi-like roll.

You may need to wet the ends of the nori sheet so it stays together. With a sharp knife carefully slice into 5 rolls about 1 ½" wide.

Repeat for the second sheet of nori. Serve rolls immediately with spicy peanut dipping sauce.

Chickpea & Sun Dried Tomato Bruschetta w/Balsamic Glaze

PREP TIME: 15 minutes • **COOK TIME:** 10 minutes • **MAKES:** 10 pieces

So simple yet so flavorful and delicious! A perfect appetizer that everyone will love!

1 cup chickpeas, cooked and drained
3 tablespoons water
1 tablespoon parsley, finely chopped
2 tablespoons sun dried tomatoes, finely chopped
½ teaspoon olive oil
1 teaspoon lemon juice
1 teaspoon minced garlic
¼ teaspoon salt
⅛ teaspoon pepper
1 French style baguette

BALSAMIC GLAZE
¼ cup balsamic vinegar
1 tablespoon agave syrup

Add chickpeas and water to a food processor and pulse until chickpeas are broken apart and appear flaked.

Transfer mashed chickpeas to a large bowl along with fresh parsley, sun dried tomatoes, olive oil, lemon juice, minced garlic, salt and pepper. Mix well then place in refrigerator.

Cut baguette into 10 thick slices and toast on a grill or in a hot skillet until browned on both sides.

Prepare glaze by adding balsamic vinegar and agave syrup to a small sauce pan and simmer on medium/low about 5 minutes until it starts to thicken.

Top toasted bread with chickpea mixture then drizzle with balsamic glaze.

Soups & Stews

30-Minute Black Bean Soup

PREP TIME: 5 minutes • **COOK TIME:** 30 minutes • **MAKES:** 8 large bowls

Black beans, tomatoes, carrots and onions are simmered in the perfect blend of spices to make this one-pot, ridiculously easy, quick and delicious soup!

- 2 tablespoons olive oil
- 3 tablespoons minced garlic
- 1 white onion, diced
- 4 carrots, diced
- 3 (15oz) cans black beans, do not drain
- 1 (15oz) can diced tomatoes, do not drain
- ½ cup tomato sauce
- 2 vegetable bouillon cubes
- 2 teaspoons sugar
- 1 teaspoon cumin
- ½ teaspoon smoked paprika
- ½ teaspoon oregano
- ¼ teaspoon chili powder
- ½ teaspoon salt
- ¼ teaspoon pepper

Heat the olive oil in a large pot over medium heat, then add the minced garlic, onion and carrots and cook 5 minutes, stirring frequently.

Add remaining ingredients to the pot and mix well to combine. Lower heat, cover and simmer for 20 minutes.

Remove from heat. Taste and adjust seasonings as desired.

The soup is a great meal on its own or serve with bread or over rice!

Wild Rice & Mushroom Soup

PREP TIME: 5 minutes • **COOK TIME:** 75 minutes • **MAKES:** 4-6 servings

Sautéed mushrooms and mixed vegetables are seasoned with fragrant spices and joined with wild rice in a thick and delicious broth. Earthy, hearty and seriously comforting, this soup takes a bit of time to come together, but it's well worth it!

- ¾ cup wild rice
- 4 tablespoons coconut oil
- ½ white onion, chopped
- 4 stalks celery, chopped
- 1 sweet potato, peeled and diced
- 3 teaspoons minced garlic
- 1 teaspoon dried thyme
- 4 cups vegetable broth
- 2 cups mushrooms, sliced
- 1 teaspoon poultry seasoning
- 1 teaspoon salt
- ½ teaspoon pepper
- 3 tablespoons vegan butter, melted
- ⅓ cup flour
- ¾ cup almond milk

In a medium saucepan bring 5 cups of water to a boil then stir in wild rice. Cover pan with a lid, then reduce heat to maintain a fast simmer, and cook for 45 minutes until the grains split open. Drain and set rice aside.

In a large pot over medium heat add coconut oil, onion, celery, sweet potato, minced garlic and thyme and sauté until vegetables are softened, about 5 minutes. Pour in vegetable broth and bring to a boil.

Add mushrooms, poultry seasoning, salt and pepper, then reduce heat and allow to simmer for about 10 minutes.

Meanwhile, in a medium bowl mix together melted vegan butter and flour, then whisk in the almond milk until you have a smooth, thickened sauce.

Pour the creamy sauce and the wild rice into the soup pot and combine thoroughly.

Allow soup to heat through, about 5 minutes. Remove from heat and let sit for a few minutes to thicken. Taste and add more seasoning if desired.

Cajun Corn & Quinoa Chowder

PREP TIME: 5 minutes • **COOK TIME:** 30 minutes • **MAKES:** 4 servings

Cozy up to a big bowl of this protein-rich vegan chowder packed with sweet corn, chickpeas, quinoa and mixed vegetables. Hearty with a cajun kick, it's a great year-round soup!

2 tablespoons olive oil
¼ large white onion, chopped
½ red bell pepper, diced
2 teaspoons minced garlic
1 teaspoon dried thyme
1 tablespoon dried parsley
2 cups vegetable broth
1 ½ cups almond milk
⅓ cup quinoa
½ cup carrots, chopped
1 ½ cups frozen sweet corn
1 ¼ cups chickpeas, cooked
1 teaspoon turmeric
2 tablespoons cajun seasoning
3 tablespoons cornstarch
salt & pepper to taste

Heat the olive oil in a pot over medium-high heat, then add the onion and bell pepper, cooking about 3-5 minutes until tender. Add garlic, thyme and parsley and cook another minute until fragrant.

Pour in vegetable broth then mix in 1 cup of the almond milk and bring to a boil.

Add quinoa, carrots, corn and chickpeas to the pot then season with turmeric and cajun seasoning, mixing well. Reduce heat to medium-low and whisk in cornstarch to thicken.

Bring to a simmer and cook uncovered for about 15 minutes until quinoa is cooked, stirring often.

Gradually mix in the remainder of the almond milk until you achieve the desired consistency then season with salt and pepper to taste.

Cheesy Broccoli & Potato Soup

PREP TIME: 10 minutes • **COOK TIME:** 30 minutes • **MAKES:** 4 servings

Chopped broccoli and potatoes simmered in a luscious non-dairy cheesy sauce. This is a simple soup that tastes anything but basic!

2 teaspoons olive oil
½ medium white onion, diced
3 cups vegetable broth
1 large potato, cubed
2 cups broccoli, chopped
½ cup cashews
¾ cup water
¼ cup nutritional yeast
2 teaspoons garlic powder
1 teaspoon paprika
salt and pepper to taste

In a large pot heat olive oil over medium heat, then add onion and sauté for about 5 minutes until slightly browned and tender.

Add in vegetable broth and potatoes. Let the liquid come to a boil, reduce heat to medium-low, then cover and simmer for 10-15 minutes until potatoes are softened.

Process cashews, water, nutritional yeast flakes, garlic powder and paprika in a blender until smooth and creamy, then add to the pot along with the broccoli.

Mix thoroughly, then cover the pot and let simmer an additional 5 minutes, stirring occasionally.

Pour half of the soup into a vented blender and process until smooth, then return to the pot and mix well (or use an immersion blender to cream half of the soup).

Remove from heat and add salt and pepper to taste. Enjoy warm.

Roasted Garlic & Asparagus Soup

PREP TIME: 5 minutes • **COOK TIME:** 25 minutes • **MAKES:** 4 servings

If you like asparagus then you will love this creamy soup! Requiring just a handful of ingredients and so easy to make, this light, bright, velvety smooth dish is a delicious lunch or a beautiful start to a wonderful dinner!

- 2 pounds fresh asparagus
- 8 garlic cloves
- 2 tablespoons olive oil
- 3 cups vegetable broth
- ½ cup coconut cream
- ½ cup almond milk
- 1 teaspoon lemon juice
- ½ teaspoon salt
- ⅛ teaspoon pepper

Preheat oven to 450 degrees F and line a baking sheet with parchment paper.

Trim and discard the ends of the asparagus, then cut in half.

Toss asparagus and garlic cloves in olive oil and sprinkle with a pinch of salt and pepper, then arrange on baking sheet in a single layer and roast for 15 minutes, stirring once.

Remove asparagus and garlic from oven and transfer to a blender. Add vegetable broth, coconut cream, almond milk and lemon juice then blend until completely smooth.

Pour soup into a large pot and warm over medium heat about 5 minutes, stirring frequently.

Mix in salt and pepper, then taste and add more seasoning if desired.

West African Peanut Stew

PREP TIME: 10 minutes • **COOK TIME:** 25 minutes • **MAKES:** 4 servings

This well-balanced sweet and savory stew delivers an abundance of nourishment with peanuts, an array of vegetables and spices. It's wonderful as a stand-alone meal or served with a grain on the side such as rice or quinoa!

- ¼ medium white onion, diced
- ½ tablespoon olive oil
- 2 teaspoons minced garlic
- ½ tablespoon minced ginger
- 1 sweet potato, peeled and cubed
- 4 cups vegetable broth
- ¾ cup peanut butter
- 3 tablespoons tomato paste
- ½ teaspoon red pepper flakes
- ½ teaspoon coriander
- ½ teaspoon cumin
- ½ teaspoon cayenne pepper
- 2 cups collard greens
- salt & pepper to taste

Add diced onion to a large soup pot over medium-high heat along with olive oil, minced garlic and ginger then sauté for 3-4 minutes. Add cubed sweet potato and mix well to combine.

Add in vegetable broth, peanut butter and tomato paste to the pot and stir until peanut butter and tomato paste are mostly dissolved into the broth. Season with red pepper flakes, coriander, cumin and cayenne pepper.

Turn the heat up to bring the stew to a boil. Let boil for a minute, then turn heat to low. Cover and simmer for 15 minutes until sweet potatoes are tender, stirring periodically.

Meanwhile, wash the collard greens thoroughly, remove the stems then roughly chop into strips.

Once the stew has simmered for 15 minutes, mix in the collard greens and simmer for another 5 minutes.

Taste stew and adjust flavor with salt and pepper to your liking.

Coconut Curry Soup

PREP TIME: 5 minutes • **COOK TIME:** 15 minutes • **MAKES:** 4 servings

Sautéed mushroom, onion, garlic and ginger are paired with rice noodles and baby corn in a coconut milk based broth. Add in a spicy kick from red curry paste and it makes for one delicious soup!

- 1 ½ tablespoons coconut oil
- 1 red bell pepper, sliced
- ½ medium white onion, chopped
- 1 cup mushrooms, sliced
- 3 garlic cloves, finely chopped
- 2 teaspoons minced ginger
- 2 ½ tablespoons red curry paste
- 4 cups vegetable broth
- 1 can (14oz) coconut milk
- 3 tablespoons soy sauce
- 2 teaspoons brown sugar
- 1 teaspoon salt
- ½ teaspoon pepper
- 1 can (15 oz) cut baby corn
- 4 oz rice noodles
- 1 tablespoon lime juice
- 2 scallions, chopped
- 1 tablespoon cilantro, chopped

In a large pot over medium-high heat add coconut oil, bell pepper and onion and sauté until onion is translucent. Add mushrooms, garlic and ginger and sauté and additional 3 minutes.

Stir in red curry paste, then mix in vegetable broth, coconut milk, soy sauce, brown sugar, salt, pepper and baby corn then turn up the heat to bring to a rolling boil.

Add rice noodles, then reduce heat and allow to simmer for 5 minutes.

Remove pot from heat and stir in lime juice and scallions. Garnish with cilantro.

Cream of Zucchini Soup

PREP TIME: 3 minutes • **COOK TIME:** 25 minutes • **MAKES:** 4 servings

One of the easiest and best ways to eat zucchini! Perfect for a quick lunch or light dinner, it's creamy and delicious, but with no cream in sight!

- 2 large zucchini
- 1 cup raw cashews
- 4 cups vegetable broth
- 2 tablespoons vegan butter
- ½ teaspoon onion powder
- ½ teaspoon salt
- ¼ teaspoon pepper

Chop off the ends of the zucchini and slice into ½" disks.

Place sliced zucchini, cashews and vegetable broth into a large pot over medium high heat and bring to a boil.

Reduce heat to low and simmer for about 20 minutes until zucchini and cashews are tender.

Remove from heat and carefully transfer the soup to a blender, then blend until completely smooth.

Return blended soup to the pot and add vegan butter, onion powder, salt and pepper and mix until well combined.

Cabbage & White Bean Soup

PREP TIME: 5 minutes • **COOK TIME:** 40 minutes • **MAKES:** 6-8 servings

Simple, hearty, and tasty! The perfect fall or winter soup to warm up to!

- 1 ½ tablespoons olive oil
- ½ red onion, chopped
- 2 large carrots, thinly sliced
- 3 tablespoons minced garlic
- 2 tablespoons Italian seasoning
- 1 teaspoon smoked paprika
- ¼ teaspoon red pepper flakes
- 1 ½ teaspoons salt
- ¼ teaspoon pepper
- 4 cups vegetable broth
- 2 cups water
- 2 cups cannellini beans, cooked and drained
- ½ head green cabbage, chopped
- 1 cup collard greens, chopped
- 1 tablespoon lemon juice
- 1 tablespoon sugar

In a large pot sauté the onion, carrots and minced garlic in olive oil over medium heat for about 5 minutes until the onion is translucent.

Add Italian seasoning, smoked paprika, red pepper flakes, salt and pepper and mix well, allowing it to cook for an additional minute.

Pour in vegetable broth and water then add the beans, cabbage and collard greens. Increase heat to bring to a rolling boil for a minute, then reduce heat to low and cover. Let simmer for 30 minutes.

Remove from heat then add lemon juice and sugar and stir until well combined.

Roasted Tomato Basil Soup

PREP TIME: 5 minutes • **COOK TIME:** 50 minutes • **MAKES:** 4 bowls

A simple healthy classic! This soup is rich, bold and flavorful with roasted tomatoes, garlic, onion and basil.

6 medium tomatoes
8 cloves garlic, peeled
2 tablespoons olive oil
1 yellow onion, sliced
1 tablespoon basil
½ tablespoon oregano
1 ¼ cups vegetable broth
¾ cup almond milk
2 tablespoons vegan butter
½ tablespoon sugar
salt & pepper to taste

Preheat oven to 400 degrees F and line a large baking sheet.

Cut tomatoes in half and place in a large bowl along with garlic cloves. Drizzle with olive oil and sprinkle generously with salt and pepper, then toss so the tomatoes and garlic are coated in oil and spices.

Transfer contents of the bowl to the baking sheet and roast in a single layer for 20 minutes.

Remove baking sheet from the oven and add the sliced onion to it, carefully tossing to coat in the liquid from the tomatoes.

Put the pan back into the oven for an additional 20 minutes.

Remove pan from the oven and transfer the contents into a blender along with basil, oregano, vegetable broth, almond milk, vegan butter and sugar then blend until smooth.

Pour the soup into a pot over low heat and simmer 10 minutes.

Taste and adjust flavor with more salt and pepper.

Hearty Lentil Stew

PREP TIME: 10 minutes • **COOK TIME:** 50 minutes • **MAKES:** 4-5 servings

Bursting to the brim with green lentils and fresh vegetables, this fiber rich stew is comfort in a bowl!

- 1 ¼ cups green lentils
- 3 ½ cups water, divided
- 2 tablespoons vegan butter
- 2 tablespoons minced garlic
- ⅓ white onion, diced
- 2 stalks celery, chopped
- 2 carrots, peeled & chopped
- 2 medium tomatoes, diced
- 1 medium potato, peeled and diced
- 1 vegetable bouillon cube
- 4 tablespoons tomato paste
- ¼ cup ketchup
- 1 teaspoon browning sauce
- 1 teaspoon salt
- ½ teaspoon pepper
- 1 tablespoon parsley, chopped

In a large pot warm the vegan butter over medium heat. Once melted, add the garlic, onion, celery and carrots and saute until fragrant and the onion is translucent, about 5 minutes.

Add the diced tomatoes and cook for 2-3 more minutes, stirring often, in order to enhance their flavor.

Pour in 3 ½ cups of water, then add the lentils, diced potato, vegetable bouillon cube, tomato paste, ketchup, browning sauce, salt and pepper to the pot and combine well, then raise heat to bring the mixture to a boil. Reduce heat to low, then cover and simmer for 40-45 minutes until lentils and potatoes are tender and fully cooked.

Garnish with chopped parsley (optional) and serve warm.

Sandwiches & Wraps

Lentil Meatball Marinara Sub

PREP TIME: 10 minutes • **COOK TIME:** 30 minutes • **MAKES:** 3 subs

Warm and comforting, flavorful oven baked lentil "meat" balls are smothered in marinara sauce and enveloped in a toasted sub roll. These are sure to be loved by all!

1 tablespoon olive oil
1 cup mushrooms, chopped
¼ large white onion, diced
1 ½ cups lentils, cooked
½ cup brown rice, cooked
⅓ cup flour
⅔ cup rolled oats
2 teaspoons Italian seasoning
2 tablespoons vegan Worcestershire sauce
2 tablespoons barbecue sauce
1 teaspoon garlic powder
1 teaspoon salt
3 sub rolls

SAUCE
2 cups marinara sauce
2 tablespoons nutritional yeast

Preheat oven to 400 degrees F and line a baking sheet with parchment paper.

Add olive oil to a skillet over medium high heat and sauté the mushrooms and onion until they are cooked down and the onion is translucent.

Transfer to a large mixing bowl then add in lentils, brown rice, flour, oats, Italian seasoning, vegan Worcestershire sauce, BBQ sauce, garlic powder and salt..

Stir to thoroughly combine, while mashing the lentils with the back of a spoon.

Form the mixture into 1 ½" balls, yielding 12-15.

Place lentil balls on the baking sheet and bake for 25 minutes, flipping half way through baking time.

Warm the marinara sauce in a large pan over medium heat, then stir in nutritional yeast flakes.

Transfer lentil balls to the pan and gently toss to fully coat with marinara sauce.

Place the lentil meatballs inside toasted sub rolls and spoon more of the heated sauce on top.

Top with vegan parmesan cheese (optional).

Mushroom BLTA Sandwich

PREP TIME: 1 hour • **COOK TIME:** 10 minutes • **MAKES:** 2 sandwiches

Smokey portobello mushroom "bacon", crisp lettuce, tomato and avocado make for an absolutely delicious BLTA sandwich.

- 2 portobello mushroom caps
- ¼ cup maple syrup
- 2 teaspoons vegan Worcestershire sauce
- 1 teaspoon liquid smoke
- ½ teaspoon smoked paprika
- ½ teaspoon salt
- ¼ teaspoon pepper
- 1 tablespoon olive oil

- 4 slices toasted bread
- 4 tablespoons vegan mayonnaise
- 1 tomato, sliced
- 1 bunch lettuce
- ½ avocado, sliced

Slice mushroom caps lengthwise into 1/2" thick pieces.

In a shallow bowl whisk together maple syrup, vegan Worcestershire sauce, liquid smoke, smoked paprika, salt and pepper.

Marinate mushrooms in the mixture for at least an hour. Flip mushrooms halfway to ensure even coverage.

Heat olive oil in a skillet over medium heat and cook marinated mushrooms for about 5 minutes on each side until browned and edges become slightly crispy.

Spread vegan mayonnaise on toasted bread and sprinkle with salt and pepper. Top with lettuce, tomato, avocado and cooked mushrooms, then cut sandwich in half diagonally.

Black Bean & Lentil BBQ Burgers

PREP TIME: 30 minutes • **COOK TIME:** 10 minutes • **MAKES:** 6 burgers

These savory delights are sturdy and meaty with black beans and lentils in every bite. They go great with just about any side dish and freeze amazingly!

- ¾ cup walnuts
- 2 cups black beans, cooked and drained
- 2 tablespoons olive oil, divided
- ½ medium white onion, diced
- ¾ cup lentils, cooked
- ½ cup Panko breadcrumbs
- ⅓ cup barbecue sauce
- 1 teaspoon ground cumin
- ½ teaspoon salt
- ½ teaspoon pepper
- ¾ cup flour
- 6 hamburger buns

Place walnuts in a food processor and blend until a coarse meal forms, then add in black beans and process until beans are broken down and slightly mushy. Transfer to a large mixing bowl and set aside.

Sauté onion in 1 tablespoon of olive oil over medium heat for about 5 minutes until soft and moderately browned. Add onions to a food processor along with lentils and pulse until a choppy mixture is achieved.

Add onion and lentil mixture to the mixing bowl along with breadcrumbs, BBQ sauce, cumin, salt and pepper then mix well. A little at a time, fold in the flour until the mixture firms up and is able to be held together.

Divide burger mixture into 6 equal parts and mold into patties. Place into the freezer for 15 minutes to allow the patties to firm up.

Cook burgers in a skillet with a tablespoon of olive oil over medium heat, or they may be grilled. Cook for about 5 minutes on each side until browned and warm throughout.

Saucy Quinoa Veggie Wrap

PREP TIME: 5 minutes • **COOK TIME:** 5 minutes • **MAKES:** 4 wraps

A colorful, flavorful wrap that comes together in a snap. Can easily be transformed into a veggie bowl by forgoing the wrap and drizzling the sauce right on top!

4 whole wheat wraps
1 cup quinoa, cooked
1 cup baby spinach
1 avocado, sliced
½ red onion, sliced thin
½ cup shredded carrots
½ cup sun-dried tomatoes

SRIRACHA DIJON SAUCE
½ cup vegan mayonnaise
2 teaspoons dijon mustard
1 teaspoon sriracha
¼ teaspoon pepper
1 tablespoon water

Add sriracha dijon sauce ingredients to a bowl and whisk together until thoroughly combined.

Divide the sauce among the wraps and spread over each wrap.

Evenly spread the quinoa over the sauce, then add spinach, avocado, onion, carrots and sun-dried tomatoes.

Fold two ends in, then roll the wrap tightly like a burrito. Slice the wrap in half diagonally and serve.

Tempeh Sloppy Joe Sandwiches

PREP TIME: 5 minutes • **COOK TIME:** 20 minutes • **MAKES:** 4 sandwiches

A simple, quick and tasty vegan take on a comfort classic made right on the stovetop!

- 1 tablespoon olive oil
- ¼ white onion, diced
- ½ green bell pepper, diced
- ½ jalapeño, finely chopped
- 2 teaspoons minced garlic
- 8 oz tempeh, crumbled
- 1 ¼ cup ketchup
- ¼ cup water
- 2 teaspoons maple syrup
- 2 teaspoons vegan Worcestershire sauce
- 1 teaspoon mustard
- 1 teaspoon chili powder
- ½ teaspoon salt
- ¼ teaspoon pepper
- 4 hamburger buns

Heat olive oil in a large skillet over medium heat then add onion, bell pepper, jalapeño and minced garlic and cook for 2 minutes, stirring frequently.

Add in crumbled tempeh, ketchup, water, maple syrup, Worcestershire sauce, mustard and seasonings and mix well.

Reduce heat to low. Cover and simmer for 17-20 minutes, stirring occasionally, until sauce has thickened and tempeh is tender.

Serve on burger buns.

Oyster Mushroom Po' Boy w/ Dill Remoulade Sauce

PREP TIME: 15 minutes • **COOK TIME:** 5 minutes • **MAKES:** 4 sandwiches

Oyster mushrooms are coated in a lightly spiced breading then fried until crisp, dressed with fresh veggies and a delicious creamy tangy sauce piled into a toasted sub roll.

20 oyster mushroom pieces, de-stemmed
⅓ cup flour
½ cup water
1 teaspoon vegan Worcestershire sauce
½ cup flour
¼ cup cornmeal
¼ Panic breadcrumbs
1 teaspoon garlic powder
1 teaspoon cumin
1 teaspoon salt

vegetable oil for frying

4 toasted split sub buns
lettuce
sliced tomato
sliced pickles

DILL REMOULADE SAUCE
¼ cup vegan mayonnaise
1 teaspoon hot sauce
½ teaspoon dried dill
1 teaspoon water

Prepare the sauce by combing vegan mayonnaise, hot sauce, dill weed and water in a small bowl. Store in refrigerator until ready to assemble sandwich.

In a medium bowl whisk together ⅓ cup flour and ½ cup water, then mix in Worcestershire sauce to form a smooth batter.

In a separate bowl combine ½ cup flour, cornmeal, breadcrumbs, garlic powder, cumin and salt.

One at a time dip the mushrooms into the wet batter then dredge into the flour mixture until well breaded.

In batches over medium high heat fry breaded mushrooms in about ¾" of vegetable oil until golden and crisp, about 5 minutes, flipping half way. Drain on paper towels.

To assemble, spread a good helping of the tangy dill sauce on the bottom side of the bun, top with 4-5 mushroom pieces, lettuce, tomato and sliced pickles and close bun. Enjoy warm.

Bang Bang Cauliflower Sandwich

PREP TIME: 10 minutes • **COOK TIME:** 35 minutes • **MAKES:** 4 sandwiches

Cauliflower steaks coated in a seasoned chickpea flour batter, baked until crispy, then slathered with bang bang sauce and served on a bun. The ultimate vegan sandwich full of flavor, crunch and spice!

1 large head cauliflower
1 cup chickpea flour
2 teaspoons nutritional yeast
1 teaspoon garlic powder
1 teaspoon onion powder
½ teaspoon pepper
½ cup water

4 sandwich buns

BANG BANG SAUCE
½ cup vegan mayonnaise
¼ cup + 2 tablespoons Thai sweet chili sauce
3 teaspoons sriracha

Preheat oven to 450 degrees F and line a baking sheet with parchment paper. Prepare cauliflower by de-stemming and from top to bottom cut into ¾ inch steaks.

In a shallow dish combine chickpea flour, nutritional yeast, garlic powder, onion powder, and pepper, then mix in water to form a batter. Submerge cauliflower steaks into the batter, then place on the baking sheet and bake for 30 minutes, flipping the cauliflower half way through.

Meanwhile, prepare the bang bang sauce by whisking together vegan mayonnaise, Thai sweet chili sauce and sriracha in a small bowl.

Once the cauliflower steaks are browned and crispy, remove from the oven and brush each side generously with the bang bang sauce. Return to the baking sheet and bake an additional 3 minutes.

Serve the cauliflower on toasted sandwich buns with your toppings of choice (lettuce, tomato and sliced avocado go great).

Spinach Mushroom Hummus Quesadillas

PREP TIME: 10 minutes • **COOK TIME:** 5 minutes • **MAKES:** 4 quesadillas

Made with hummus instead of cheese, these quesadillas are super tasty and quick - ready to go in just a few minutes! Serve with guacamole, pico de gallo or salsa to really take them over the top!

HUMMUS
- 1 ¼ cups chickpeas, cooked and drained
- ¼ cup tahini
- ⅓ cup water
- 2 tablespoons olive oil
- 2 tablespoons lemon juice
- 1 teaspoon minced garlic
- ½ teaspoon ground cumin
- ¼ teaspoon onion powder
- ½ teaspoon salt

- 8 - 8" flour tortillas
- 1 cup baby spinach
- 1 cup mushrooms, sliced
- ½ red onion, sliced

Place hummus ingredients into a blender and process until smooth.

Assemble quesadillas by spreading an even layer of hummus onto a tortilla. Top with a thin layer of spinach, mushrooms and red onion, then place another tortilla on top to cover.

Lightly grease a large skillet with oil over medium heat. Add prepared quesadilla to the pan, then place another pan on top and press down.

Cook for about 3 minutes until the underside has browned, then carefully flip and cook an additional 2 minutes until both sides are crispy and golden.

Remove from skillet and slice into 4 equal parts. Repeat for each quesadilla.

Enjoy warm.

Chickpea Salad Sandwich

PREP TIME: 15 minutes • **MAKES:** 4 sandwiches

This super quick and delicious chickpea salad sandwich is creamy and filling, and makes for an awesome on the go meal!

2 cups chickpeas, cooked
⅓ medium red onion, chopped
3 stalks celery, diced
⅓ cup vegan mayonnaise
2 teaspoons mustard
3 tablespoons dill relish
1 ½ tablespoons lemon juice
¼ teaspoon salt
¼ teaspoon seasoned salt
¼ teaspoon pepper

8 pieces toasted wheat bread

Drain and rinse chickpeas then mash with a fork, or pulse in a food processor just until beans are broken up and texture appears flaked.

Transfer chickpeas to a large bowl then add in red onion, celery, vegan mayonnaise, mustard, dill relish, lemon juice, salt, seasoned salt and pepper. Taste and adjust seasonings as desired.

Spread onto toasted bread as is or with your favorite toppings. Chickpea salad also works great in a wrap, with crackers, or topped on a salad!

Chipotle Portobello Sheet Pan Fajitas

PREP TIME: 10 minutes • **COOK TIME:** 30 minutes • **MAKES:** 4 fajitas

Portobello mushrooms and veggies are coated in a spicy mix of seasonings and roasted to perfection for a completely delicious one pan meal!

2 portobello mushroom caps
1 red bell pepper
1 yellow bell pepper
½ white onion
2 tablespoons olive oil
1 tablespoon soy sauce
1 teaspoon maple syrup
1 teaspoon chipotle powder
½ teaspoon chili powder
½ teaspoon garlic powder
1 teaspoon cumin
½ teaspoon salt

4 small flour tortillas

AVOCADO TOPPING
1 avocado, mashed
1 teaspoon lemon juice
½ teaspoon onion powder
¼ teaspoon salt
1 tablespoon water

Preheat oven to 400 degrees F.

Slice the mushrooms and peppers into long ¼" wide strips and chop the onion, then transfer to a large mixing bowl.

Add olive oil, soy sauce, maple syrup, chipotle powder, chili powder, garlic powder, cumin and salt to a small bowl then mix well. Pour the seasoning mix over the vegetables and gently toss until everything is well coated in oil and spices.

Pour the contents of the mixing bowl onto a baking sheet, arranging the vegetables in a single layer then roast for 25-30 minutes until the vegetables are slightly wilted and the edges have browned. Turn halfway through cooking time.

Meanwhile prepare the avocado topping by mixing together mashed avocado, lemon juice, onion powder, salt and water.

Equally scoop the roasted vegetables into each tortilla, then top with the avocado mixture.

Crispy Falafel Pita Wraps

PREP TIME: 40 minutes • **COOK TIME:** 5 minutes • **MAKES:** 3 wraps

Crisp and browned on the outside, warm and soft on the inside, falafel are stuffed into a pita and topped with a simple tahini sauce.

FALAFEL
1 ½ cups chickpeas, cooked and drained
¼ white onion, chopped
3 cloves garlic
¼ cup parsley, fresh
4 tablespoons flour
1 teaspoon lemon juice
1 teaspoon salt
1 ½ teaspoon cumin
1 teaspoon coriander

vegetable oil for frying

TAHINI SAUCE
3 tablespoons tahini
1 ½ teaspoon lemon juice
⅛ teaspoon salt
2 tablespoons water

FOR THE WRAPS
3 pita wraps
½ cup mixed greens
1 large tomato, sliced
⅓ red onion, sliced

Place falafel ingredients into a food processor and pulse until just combined and mostly smooth. Refrigerate for 30 minutes.

Shape the falafel dough into 1 ½" balls, yielding about 12-15.

Fill a skillet with about ½" of vegetable oil and heat over medium-high heat.

Once shimmering, place falafel balls into the oil and fry until golden brown, turning throughout to ensure even browning.

Place on a paper towel lined plate to absorb excess oil.

In a small bowl whisk together tahini sauce ingredients.

Warm the pita bread and fill with mixed greens, tomato, onion and falafel. Drizzle tahini sauce generously on top.

Blackened Tofu Caesar Wraps

PREP TIME: 10 minutes • **COOK TIME:** 50 minutes • **MAKES:** 4 wraps

These wraps are pretty dang amazing! "Meaty" blackened tofu is perfectly paired with crisp lettuce, coconut bacon and vegan caesar dressing.

COCONUT BACON
- ⅓ cup unsweetened coconut flakes
- ½ tablespoon olive oil
- ½ tablespoon liquid smoke
- ½ tablespoon soy sauce
- ½ tablespoon maple syrup
- ½ tablespoon apple cider vinegar
- ¼ teaspoon smoked paprika

BLACKENED TOFU
- 1 (16 oz) block extra firm tofu
- 2 tablespoons olive oil
- 3 tablespoons mustard
- 1 ½ teaspoons smoked paprika
- 1 teaspoon cumin
- 1 teaspoon thyme
- ½ teaspoon salt
- ¼ teaspoon pepper

WRAPS
- 4 large flour tortillas
- 1 cups romaine lettuce, chopped
- 1 avocado, sliced
- 1 tomato, sliced
- ½ cup vegan caesar dressing

Preheat oven to 325 degrees F. In a bowl mix together all of the ingredients for the coconut bacon. Spread evenly on a parchment lined baking sheet and bake about 15 minutes, stirring every few minutes until lightly browned and crispy. Remove from oven and let cool.

Next increase oven temperature to 400 degrees F. In a large bowl mix together olive oil and mustard until well combined. Press the tofu then cut into bite sized cubes. Place the tofu into the bowl and gently toss with oil and mustard mixture to coat.

In a small bowl whisk together smoked paprika, cumin, thyme, salt and pepper. Sprinkle half of the spice mix over the tofu, toss, then sprinkle on remaining spice mix and toss again. Place tofu on parchment lined baking sheet and bake for 20 minutes. Remove from oven and flip each piece, then bake for an additional 15 minutes until crispy.

Divide the blackened tofu between the 4 tortillas, making a mound in the center. Top with lettuce, avocado, tomato and sprinkle on the coconut bacon. Drizzle with vegan caesar dressing and roll burrito style. Cut in half and serve.

Side Dishes

Old Bay Potato Wedges w/ Smoked Buffalo Dipping Sauce

PREP TIME: 10 minutes • **COOK TIME:** 40 minutes • **MAKES:** 3 servings

Crispy homemade wedges without frying! Oven baked spuds are paired with a simple yet flavor-packed spicy dipping sauce that takes them out of this world!

4 medium russet potatoes
1 tablespoon flour
1 ½ teaspoons Old Bay seasoning
1 teaspoon salt
½ teaspoon pepper
1 teaspoon olive oil

SMOKED BUFFALO SAUCE
⅓ cup vegan mayonnaise
2 ½ teaspoons sriracha
½ teaspoon smoked paprika

Preheat oven to 425 degrees F.

Wash potatoes then cut each potato in half lengthwise. Cut each half into 4 wedges to get 8 wedges from each potato.

Blot potatoes with paper towels to absorb excess moisture then add wedges to a large mixing bowl.

Sprinkle flour, Old Bay seasoning and salt and pepper over potatoes then drizzle with olive oil and toss everything together to coat.

Arrange potatoes in a single layer on a parchment lined baking sheet and bake for about 40 minutes until browned, crisp and cooked through, flipping wedges halfway into baking time.

While wedges are baking, make the smoked buffalo dipping sauce by combining the vegan mayonnaise, sriracha and smoked paprika.

Allow potatoes to cool for about 3 minutes then enjoy with dipping sauce.

Pan-Steamed Garlic Kale

PREP TIME: 5 minutes • **COOK TIME:** 20 minutes • **MAKES:** 2-3 servings

Sautéed, then pan-steamed this garlicky kale with a zest of lemon is melt-in-your-mouth tender and are an excellent complement to any main dish!

1 ½ tablespoon olive oil
½ white onion, finely chopped
2 ½ teaspoons minced garlic
¼ teaspoon red pepper flakes
¼ cup vegetable broth
¼ teaspoon salt
1 pound kale, stemmed and chopped
1 ½ tablespoons lemon juice
salt and pepper to taste

Add olive oil to a large pot over medium heat. Once shimmering, add onion and sauté until soft and lightly browned, about 5 minutes.

Stir in minced garlic and red pepper flakes and cook an additional minute, then stir in vegetable broth and ¼ teaspoon salt.

Add kale and toss until it begins to wilt, about 5 minutes.

Cover, reduce heat to low and simmer, stirring occasionally for 5 minutes.

Uncover and increase heat to medium and cook, stirring occasionally until kale is tender and most liquid is evaporated, about 5 minutes.

Remove from heat, stir in lemon juice and season with salt and pepper to taste.

Stir Fried Broccoli & Shiitake Mushrooms

PREP TIME: 5 minutes • **COOK TIME:** 10 minutes • **MAKES:** 2-3 servings

Easy, delicious and quick! Broccoli and shiitake mushrooms are tossed with a savory soy-based sauce and topped with scallions.

- 2 tablespoons water
- 1 tablespoon soy sauce
- 1 tablespoon dry sherry
- 2 tablespoons brown sugar
- 2 teaspoons minced ginger
- 1 teaspoon toasted sesame oil
- 1 tablespoon olive oil
- 2 ½ cups broccoli florets
- 1 cup shiitake mushrooms, sliced
- 1 teaspoon lemon juice
- salt and pepper to taste
- 2 scallions, sliced thin

Add water, soy sauce, dry sherry, brown sugar, ginger and sesame oil to a bowl and whisk until well combined. Set aside.

Heat olive oil in a skillet over medium-high heat, then add broccoli and sliced mushrooms and cook, stirring occasionally, about 5 minutes until broccoli starts to brown.

Pour in soy sauce mixture and toss vegetables to coat. Cook an additional 2 minutes.

Add lemon juice and add salt and pepper to taste. Mix well.

Transfer to platter and sprinkle with scallions.

Cheesy Spinach Rice

PREP TIME: 5 minutes • **COOK TIME:** 45 minutes • **MAKES:** 4-6 servings

This brown rice one-pot recipe makes the perfect side dish using fresh spinach!

3 tablespoons olive oil
1 onion, finely chopped
1 teaspoon salt
¼ teaspoon pepper
1 ½ cups long-grain brown rice
2 teaspoons minced garlic
1 teaspoon dried oregano
2 ½ cups vegetable broth
2 cups spinach
2 scallions, thinly sliced
1 tablespoon lemon juice
salt and pepper to taste

PINE NUT COTIJA CHEESE
½ cup pine nuts
1 ½ tablespoons nutritional yeast
½ tablespoon garlic powder
¼ teaspoon salt

Heat olive oil in a large saucepan over medium heat. Add onion, salt and pepper and sauté for about 5 minutes until softened.

Add rice and stir frequently until edges begin to turn translucent, about 3 minutes. Add minced garlic and oregano and cook an additional minute.

Stir in vegetable broth and increase heat to bring to a rolling boil. Cover, reduce heat to low and cook until liquid is absorbed and rice is tender, about 25-30 minutes.

While the rice is cooking prepare pine nut Cotija cheese by placing pine nuts, nutritional yeast, garlic powder and salt in a food processor and and pulsing until a fine meal is formed. Set aside.

Turn off heat, stir in spinach, then cover and let sit for 5 minutes. Uncover and fluff rice. Add scallions and lemon juice then toss.

Taste and season with salt and pepper. Transfer to platter and sprinkle with pine nut cotija cheese blend.

Old-Fashioned Potato Salad

PREP TIME: 10 minutes • **COOK TIME:** 10 minutes • **MAKES:** 6 servings

This creamy potato salad has just the right amount of tang and savoriness. A perfect side dish for any party or barbecue!

6 medium russet potatoes
¼ medium red onion, diced
2 stalks celery, chopped
¾ cup vegan mayonnaise
2 teaspoons vinegar
2 teaspoons mustard
¼ cup dill relish
1 teaspoon celery seed
1 teaspoon onion powder
1 teaspoon salt
¼ teaspoon pepper
1 teaspoon parsley flakes
½ teaspoon paprika

Peel and cut potatoes into bite sized chunks. Place into a large pot and cover with water. Bring the water to a boil and cook about 10 minutes until the potatoes are fork tender.

Drain and allow the potatoes to cool for at least 15 minutes.

In a large mixing bowl add the remaining ingredients and mix well to combine.

Add potatoes and toss gently to coat.

Cover and refrigerate for at least 2 hours to allow the flavors to blend.

Roasted Brussels Sprouts w/ Agave Mustard Glaze

PREP TIME: 5 minutes • **COOK TIME:** 20 minutes • **MAKES:** 2-3 servings

Crispy oven roasted Brussels sprouts dressed with a tangy mustard glaze are a quick and easy hands-off side dish. Beware, these are shockingly addictive!

3 cups brussels sprouts, trimmed and halved
1 teaspoons olive oil
½ teaspoon salt
½ teaspoon pepper
1 ½ tablespoons toasted almonds, sliced

AGAVE MUSTARD GLAZE
2 tablespoons mustard
1 tablespoon fresh sage, finely chopped
1 tablespoon apple cider vinegar
2 teaspoons agave nectar
2 teaspoons olive oil
½ teaspoon salt
½ teaspoon pepper

Preheat oven to 450 degrees F.

In a large bowl toss Brussels sprouts with olive oil, salt and pepper then spread evenly in a singer layer on a parchment lined baking sheet.

Roast for 20 minutes until sprouts are browned with a crispy outer layer, flipping sprouts over halfway through baking time.

While sprouts are in the oven prepare the glaze by mixing together mustard, fresh sage, apple cider vinegar, agave nectar, olive oil, salt and pepper.

Once out of the oven drizzle glaze over Brussels sprouts and sprinkle with toasted almonds.

Mexican Street Corn Salad

PREP TIME: 5 minutes • **COOK TIME:** 30 minutes • **MAKES:** 4 servings

Creamy, spicy, tangy and delicious- this side dish has it all! A simple vegan take on the traditional flavors of Mexican street corn.

CORN SALAD
- 3 cups yellow corn, cooked
- ¼ cup vegan mayonnaise
- 1 ½ tablespoons cilantro, finely chopped
- 1 green onion stalk, finely chopped
- ¼ cup red onion, diced
- 1 tablespoon lime juice
- 1 teaspoon hot sauce
- 1 teaspoon chili powder
- ¼ teaspoon salt
- ⅛ teaspoon pepper

PINE NUT COTIJA
- ⅓ cup pine nuts
- 2 tablespoons nutritional yeast
- ½ tablespoon garlic powder
- ½ teaspoon salt

Place all ingredients for the corn salad into a large bowl and mix until well combined.

Add pine nuts, nutritional yeast, garlic powder and salt to a food processor and pulse until a fine meal is achieved.

Stir the pine nut Cotija cheese mixture into the corn salad bowl. Taste and adjust seasonings if necessary.

Balsamic Roasted Tahini Carrots

PREP TIME: 5 minutes • **COOK TIME:** 30 minutes • **MAKES:** 4 servings

Sweet and savory, these delicious maple-balsamic glazed carrots are an easy side dish great with any meal!

- 4 large carrots
- 2 ½ tablespoons balsamic vinegar
- 2 tablespoons olive oil
- 2 tablespoons maple syrup
- ½ teaspoon red pepper flakes
- ¼ teaspoon salt
- ⅛ teaspoon pepper
- 2 tablespoons tahini

Preheat oven to 400 degrees F and line a baking sheet with parchment paper.

Peel carrots and cut off the ends, then slice into ¼" diagonal disks. Transfer to a large bowl.

In a small bowl whisk together the balsamic vinegar, olive oil, maple syrup, red pepper flakes, salt and pepper. Pour the mixture over the carrots and toss to coat.

Arrange carrots on the baking sheet in a single layer, pouring the remaining liquid on top.

Roast 30 minutes until the carrots are fork tender and slightly charred, turning half way through cooking time.

Remove from oven and drizzle with tahini.

Cheesy Stovetop Macaroni

PREP TIME: 5 minutes • **COOK TIME:** 15 minutes • **MAKES:** 4 servings

A tasty ode to a childhood favorite! Macaroni noodles in a creamy cashew-based cheesy sauce simply made in just one pot and ready in only 15 minutes!

Ingredients
1 ½ cups elbow noodles, dry
1 medium carrot, peeled
½ cup raw cashews
¼ cup nutritional yeast
2 tablespoons vegan butter
2 teaspoons vinegar
½ tablespoon salt
¼ teaspoon pepper
½ teaspoon garlic powder
½ teaspoon onion powder
¼ teaspoon nutmeg
¼ cup vegetable broth
½ cup water

Place elbow noodles into a large pot, cover with water and boil for 13 minutes. Drain and return the noodles to the pot.

While the noodles are cooking, boil the carrot in a small pot of water for about 5 minutes until soft.

Once the carrot is tender remove it from the pot and add to a blender along with cashews, nutritional yeast, vegan butter, vinegar, salt, pepper, garlic powder, onion powder, nutmeg, vegetable broth and water, then blend until completely smooth and a creamy sauce forms.

Add the cheesy sauce to the pot of drained noodles and stir over medium heat until warm throughout and the noodles are well coated, about 2 minutes.

Remove from heat. Taste and add more salt if desired.

Herbed Garlic Smashed Red Potatoes

PREP TIME: 5 minutes • **COOK TIME:** 45 minutes • **MAKES:** 4 servings

No boring potatoes here! Fluffy on the inside, crispy on the outside, and smothered in garlic butter and rosemary these spuds are sure to impress!

8 small red potatoes
3 tablespoons vegan butter, melted
1 tablespoon minced garlic
½ teaspoon crushed rosemary
¼ teaspoon salt
⅛ teaspoon pepper
olive oil

Place potatoes into a large pot filled with water and boil for 25 minutes until potatoes are tender and easily pierced with a fork. Drain.

Meanwhile, preheat oven to 425 degrees F and line a baking sheet.

Arrange potatoes onto the baking sheet and press down on the center of each potato using a heavy drinking glass or a fork until it splits open and slightly flattens.

Mix together the melted vegan butter, garlic and rosemary then pour evenly on top of the potatoes.

Sprinkle evenly with salt and pepper and lightly spray with olive oil.

Bake for 20 minutes until tops turn golden brown and the skins are slightly crispy.

Easy Summertime Slaw

PREP TIME: 10 minutes • **COOK TIME:** 1 hour • **MAKES:** 8 servings

Crunchy, creamy, sweet and tangy this coleslaw is an easy classic and a must for summertime. It's an all around awesome side dish for anything grilled!

- ¾ cup vegan mayonnaise
- 2 teaspoons sugar
- 2 tablespoons apple cider vinegar
- 1 teaspoon celery seed
- 1 teaspoon mustard
- 1 teaspoon seasoned salt
- 4 cups green cabbage, shredded
- 2 ½ cups purple cabbage, shredded
- 1 1/2 cups carrot, shredded

Stir together vegan mayonnaise, sugar, vinegar, celery seed, mustard and seasoned salt in a small bowl until fully combined.

Add green cabbage, purple cabbage and carrots to a large bowl and mix well. Pour in the dressing and toss to coat thoroughly.

Cover and refrigerate for at least one hour or until ready to serve. Stir before serving.

Kung Pao Cabbage

PREP TIME: 5 minutes • **COOK TIME:** 45 minutes • **MAKES:** 4 servings

Cabbage sautéed and slow cooked until tender, tossed with a spicy Asian-inspired sauce, and topped with roasted peanuts. Doesn't get much tastier than this!

- 4 tablespoons olive oil
- 1 medium head of cabbage, trimmed, cored and chopped
- ½ white onion, diced
- ½ teaspoon salt
- ¼ teaspoon pepper
- ¼ cup soy sauce
- 1 teaspoon rice vinegar
- 1 tablespoon minced ginger
- 1 teaspoon cornstarch
- 2 teaspoons minced garlic
- ½ teaspoon red pepper flakes
- ¼ cup roasted peanuts, crushed

Heat 3 tablespoons of olive oil in a large pot over medium heat until shimmering. Add chopped cabbage and diced onion then toss to coat.

Add salt and pepper and sauté until the cabbage begins to soften, about 10 minutes.

At this point the cabbage should have released its water. If it hasn't add ¼ cup of water to keep the pan from drying. Reduce heat to low, cover and simmer, stirring occasionally, for 20 minutes.

Remove lid and let the cabbage and onions continue to cook over low heat for an additional 10 minutes, then drain any remaining liquid.

In a medium bowl whisk together soy sauce, rice vinegar, minced ginger and cornstarch, then set aside. In a small saucepan over medium heat add remaining 1 tablespoon of olive oil, minced garlic and red pepper flakes and stir until fragrant, about 1 minute.

Add the soy sauce mixture to the saucepan and stir for about 2 minutes until sauce begins to thicken. Pour sauce over cabbage and toss to coat.

Transfer to a platter and sprinkle crushed peanuts on top. Add a little more red pepper flakes for an extra kick (optional).

Garden Pasta Salad

PREP TIME: 15 minutes • **COOK TIME:** 1 hour • **MAKES:** 4-5 servings

A go-to for hot days…or any other day! Packed with crisp veggies, this cool pasta salad makes for a tasty side dish or pile it on and serve for lunch or a light dinner!

- 2 ⅔ cups tricolor rotini noodles
- ½ red bell pepper, chopped
- 2 stalks celery, chopped
- ½ red onion, diced
- 1 large carrot, peeled & diced
- 1 large tomato, diced
- ½ cucumber, diced

DRESSING
- ½ cup vegan mayonnaise
- 2 tablespoons apple cider vinegar
- 1 teaspoon dijon mustard
- 1 teaspoon maple syrup
- ½ teaspoon red pepper flakes
- ½ teaspoon salt
- ¼ teaspoon pepper

Add rotini noodles to a large pot and cover with water. Boil for 15 minutes, then drain and rinse with cold water to cool.

While the pasta is boiling, prepare the dressing by whisking together vegan mayonnaise, apple cider vinegar, dijon mustard, maple syrup, red pepper flakes, salt and pepper until completely blended and smooth.

In a large bowl add rotini noodles, bell pepper, celery, red onion, carrot, tomato and cucumber. Pour dressing on top and toss well to combine.

Cover and refrigerate at least an hour to allow flavors to blend. Taste and add more salt and pepper if desired.

Keep chilled until ready to serve.

Main Dishes

Kickin' Cajun Pasta w/ Sun Dried Tomatoes

COOK TIME: 25 minutes • **MAKES:** 3-4 servings

One of my all time go-to meals! Penne pasta in a creamy cajun sauce loaded with sun-dried tomatoes and spinach makes an easy dinner with just the right amount of kick!

CASHEW SAUCE
- ⅓ cup cashews, raw
- ½ teaspoon garlic powder
- ¼ teaspoon sea salt
- 1 ½ tablespoons nutritional yeast
- 1 cup almond milk

- 2 cups penne pasta, dry
- 2 teaspoons olive oil
- 3 teaspoons minced garlic
- ½ cup sun dried tomatoes, chopped
- 2 cups spinach, fresh
- 2 teaspoons cajun seasoning
- ⅛ teaspoon pepper

Place pasta noodles into a large pot, cover with water and boil for 13 minutes. Drain and set aside pasta once it has cooked.

Meanwhile, make the cashew sauce by adding raw cashews, garlic powder, salt, nutritional yeast flakes and almond milk into a blender and processing until smooth and creamy. Set aside.

In a large pan add olive oil, minced garlic and sun dried tomatoes then sauté over medium heat until garlic has lightly browned, about 3 minutes.

Pour in cashew sauce and stir often until it starts to thicken, about 2-3 minutes. Reduce heat to low then add in spinach and pasta and mix well.

After a minute or two the spinach should be tender. Sprinkle in the cajun seasoning and pepper and thoroughly combine.

Remove pan from heat. Taste and add more seasoning if desired.

Roasted Red Pepper & Broccoli Fettuccini Alfredo

PREP TIME: 5 minutes • **COOK TIME:** 20 minutes • **MAKES:** 4 servings

Fettuccini pasta and roasted vegetables all brought together in a ridiculously flavorful miso cream sauce makes for the perfect dinner. This decadent plant-based take on traditional fettuccini alfredo is sure to please!

6 oz fettuccini noodles, dry
2 ½ cups broccoli florets
1 red bell pepper, sliced
1 shallot, chopped
1 tablespoon olive oil
1 ½ tablespoon vegan butter
1 ½ tablespoon flour
1 ¼ cup almond milk
2 tablespoons white miso paste
¼ teaspoon thyme
1 teaspoon salt, divided
½ teaspoon pepper, divided

Preheat oven to 375 degrees F.

Toss broccoli, red pepper and shallot in olive oil, sprinkle with ¼ teaspoon of both salt and pepper and place in a single layer on a parchment lined baking sheet. Roast for 15 minutes, stirring the vegetables half way through cooking time.

Meanwhile, cook pasta according to package instructions. Drain and set aside.

Melt vegan butter in a large skillet over medium-high heat. Sprinkle in flour and whisk until dissolved. Add milk and miso paste and whisk again until smooth.

Reduce heat and bring to a simmer, then cook for 2-3 minutes until sauce begins to thicken, stirring periodically.

Mix in thyme and the remaining salt and pepper, then add cooked pasta and roasted vegetables and toss to coat with the sauce.

Remove from heat. Taste and adjust seasonings as desired.

Southwestern Quinoa Stuffed Peppers

PREP TIME: 25 minutes • **COOK TIME:** 25 minutes • **MAKES:** 6 servings

These perfectly spiced quinoa, bean and veggie stuffed peppers topped with a delicious cashew sauce make for a well rounded, nutrient-packed meal!

3 medium bell peppers, cut in half lengthwise
½ cup quinoa, dry
1 cup vegetable broth
1 teaspoon olive oil
¼ cup yellow onion, chopped
1 ½ teaspoon minced garlic
½ cup frozen corn
½ cup black beans, cooked & drained
½ cup diced tomatoes, drained
¼ teaspoon chili powder
½ teaspoon cumin
¼ teaspoon garlic powder
¼ teaspoon salt

SRIRACHA CASHEW SAUCE
½ cup raw cashews
¼ cup water
1 tablespoon sriracha
1 tablespoon lemon juice
1 teaspoon minced garlic
1 tablespoon nutritional yeast

In a medium saucepan bring 1 cup of vegetable broth to a boil, then stir in ½ cup dry quinoa. Reduce to simmer, cover and cook until grain is translucent and tender, about 15 minutes.

Preheat oven to 375 degrees F.

In a large skillet over medium heat add olive oil, onion and minced garlic and sauté until garlic begins to brown, 3-5 minutes.

Add corn, black beans and diced tomatoes and cook an additional 3 minutes. Transfer to a large mixing bowl and add cooked quinoa, chili powder, cumin, garlic powder and salt. Mix well to combine.

Fill halved bell peppers with the quinoa mixture, then place on a lined baking sheet and bake 20-25 minutes until peppers are soft.

Meanwhile prepare sauce by placing cashews, water, sriracha, lemon juice, minced garlic and nutritional yeast into a blender and processing until smooth.

Once peppers are done, top with a drizzle of sauce.

Salisbury Lentil Steaks

PREP TIME: 10 minutes • **COOK TIME:** 45 minutes • **MAKES:** 4 Salisbury steaks

Hearty lentil "steaks" are smothered in a mushroom and onion gravy for an absolutely satisfying dish!

LENTIL STEAKS
1 tablespoon olive oil
1 cup mushrooms, chopped
¼ white onion, diced
1 ½ cups lentils, cooked & drained
½ cup brown rice, cooked & drained
⅓ cup flour
⅔ cup quick oats
2 teaspoons Italian seasoning
2 tablespoons vegan Worcestershire
2 tablespoons barbecue sauce
1 teaspoon garlic powder
1 teaspoon salt

MUSHROOM GRAVY
1 ½ cups mushrooms, chopped
1 tablespoon olive oil
¼ white onion, chopped
1 teaspoon minced garlic
1 ½ tablespoons flour
1 ½ cups vegetable broth
½ teaspoon vegan Worcestershire sauce

Preheat oven to 400 degrees F and line a baking sheet with parchment paper.

Add olive oil to a skillet over medium high heat and sauté the mushrooms and onion for about 5 minutes until they are cooked down and the onion is translucent.

Transfer to a large mixing bowl and add in the remaining ingredients for the lentil steaks. Stir to thoroughly combine, while mashing the lentils with the back of a spoon.

Form the mixture into 4 patties. Place onto a baking sheet and bake for 25 minutes, flipping half way through baking time.

Meanwhile, prepare the mushroom gravy by placing mushrooms into a large pan over medium heat along with olive oil, onion and garlic. Sauté for about 5 minutes until vegetables have softened.

Stir in the flour until completely mixed in with the vegetables. Next, whisk in vegetable broth and Worcestershire sauce, scraping up all the browned bits from the bottom of the pan. Reduce heat and simmer about 3 minutes until gravy starts to thicken. Add salt and pepper to taste.

Remove pan from heat. Transfer lentil steaks to the pan and cover completely with gravy.

Smoky Chickpea + Black Bean Meatloaf

PREP TIME: 15 minutes • **COOK TIME:** 45 minutes • **MAKES:** 6 servings

Even meat eaters will love this smoky and delicious hearty meat-less loaf!

1 cup chickpeas, cooked and drained
1 cup black beans, cooked and drained
1 tablespoon olive oil
½ white onion, diced
1 cup Panko breadcrumbs
2 teaspoons nutritional yeast
¼ cup ketchup
2 tablespoons vegan Worcestershire sauce
1 ½ teaspoons liquid smoke
1 teaspoon Italian seasoning
½ teaspoon salt
⅛ teaspoon pepper

GLAZE
⅓ cup ketchup
1 teaspoon maple syrup

Preheat oven to 400 degrees F and line an 8" loaf pan with parchment paper.

Add the chickpeas and black beans to a food processor, then pulse a few times just until the beans are broken up and appear flaked. Transfer to a large bowl.

Heat olive oil in a large skillet over medium-high heat. Add onion and cook, stirring occasionally for about 5 minutes, until translucent.

To the chickpea/black bean bowl add sautéed onion, breadcrumbs, nutritional yeast, ketchup, vegan Worcestershire sauce, liquid smoke, Italian seasoning, salt and pepper. Mix until well combined.

Spoon mixture into the prepared loaf pan and press until it's evenly distributed throughout. Cover with foil and bake for 35 minutes.

While the loaf bakes, stir glaze ingredients together in a small bowl.

Remove foil, spread maple glaze evenly on top of the loaf and bake for another 10 minutes, uncovered. Let cool at least 20 minutes before serving.

Pasta Primavera Bake

PREP TIME: 5 minutes • **COOK TIME:** 55 minutes • **MAKES:** 8 servings

Filling and satisfying this veggie packed pasta dish is a perfect meal-in-one all year round!

- 1 (1lb) package rigatoni noodles
- ½ cup carrots, sliced thin
- ½ red bell pepper, cut into thin strips
- ½ green bell pepper, cut into thin strips
- 1 large tomato, diced
- 1 (24oz) jar pasta sauce
- 1 cup vegetable broth
- ½ cup almond milk
- 1 tablespoon nutritional yeast
- ¼ teaspoon dried thyme
- 1 teaspoon garlic powder
- ½ teaspoon salt
- ⅛ teaspoon pepper

Preheat oven to 400 degrees F.

Fill a large pot with water and bring to a boil. Add rigatoni noodles and sliced carrots and boil for 15 minutes. Drain and return to pot.

Add remaining ingredients to the pot and mix well to combine. Transfer to a 9x13" baking dish and cover tightly with foil. Bake for 40 minutes.

Remove from oven and allow to cool at least 10 minutes before serving.

Herbed Vegetable Pot Pies

PREP TIME: 15 minutes • **COOK TIME:** 15 minutes • **MAKES:** 4 pot pies

Packed to the brim with an array of mixed vegetables and finished with a creamy herbed sauce, these hearty pies are just downright incredible!

- 1 medium potato
- 1 tablespoon olive oil
- ¼ cup white onion, diced
- 2 teaspoons minced garlic
- 1 stalk celery, diced
- ½ cup vegetable broth
- 1 vegetable bouillon cube
- ¾ cup frozen mixed vegetables
- ½ cup mushrooms, roughly chopped
- 1 ½ cups almond milk
- 2 teaspoons cornstarch
- ½ teaspoon pepper
- 1 teaspoon rosemary
- 4 pieces vegan-friendly crescent roll dough
- 1 teaspoon vegan butter, melted

Preheat oven to 375 degrees F.

Peel potato and cut into small cubes. Place in a pot with enough water to cover them and boil for 5 minutes until tender. Drain and set aside.

In a large pan over medium heat add olive oil, onion, garlic and celery and sauté for 5 minutes.

Add vegetable broth and vegetable bouillon cube. Break up bouillon cube with a spatula and mix well to dissolve.

Next add frozen mixed vegetables, mushrooms, potatoes and almond milk and cook for about 3 minutes until mixed vegetables have softened.

In a small bowl, mix cornstarch with 2 teaspoons of water then add to the pan. Stir until sauce has thickened, about 3 minutes. Season with pepper and rosemary and combine well.

Pour vegetable mixture equally into 4 ramekins. For each ramekin take 1 piece of crescent roll dough and gently stretch it out to cover the top of the ramekin completely. Press the edges of the dough around the sides of the ramekin to secure.

Brush the surface of the dough with vegan butter then bake for about 15 minutes until biscuit tops are golden brown and cooked through.

General Tso's Cauliflower

PREP TIME: 10 minutes • **COOK TIME:** 20 minutes • **MAKES:** 2 servings

Crispy fried pieces of cauliflower are coated in a sweet- savory General Tso's style sauce made from scratch. A delicious dish that gives the taste of takeout right from your own kitchen!

FOR THE CAULIFLOWER
½ **head of cauliflower, cut into florets**
¼ **cup flour**
¼ **cup cornstarch**
¼ **teaspoon baking powder**
2 **teaspoons toasted sesame seeds**
½ **cup water**
½ **teaspoon sesame oil**
vegetable oil for frying
1 **scallion, sliced**

SAUCE
1 ½ **teaspoons sesame oil**
1 ½ **teaspoons minced garlic**
1 **teaspoon minced ginger**
¼ **cup ketchup**
¼ **cup vegetable broth**
2 **teaspoons brown sugar**
½ **teaspoon red pepper flakes**
2 **tablespoons soy sauce**
1 **teaspoon cornstarch**

In a large bowl mix together flour, cornstarch, baking powder and sesame seeds. Pour in water and mix until smooth. Add sesame oil and stir until thoroughly combined with the batter.

Place cauliflower florets into the bowl and toss until well coated.

Add about 1" of oil into a large pan and bring oil to high heat. When oil is heated reduced to medium-high and add battered cauliflower pieces, being sure not to overcrowd the pan.

Working in batches, fry cauliflower for about 5 minutes, flipping halfway, until golden brown and crispy. Remove from oil and place on a paper towel-lined plate to absorb excess oil.

To make the sauce combine sesame oil, minced garlic and minced ginger in a large skillet and cook for 2 minutes over medium heat. Add ketchup, vegetable broth, brown sugar, red pepper flakes and soy sauce, then whisk in cornstarch until sauce starts to thicken, about a minute.

Transfer the fried cauliflower into the skillet and toss until it is evenly coated with sauce, then allow to simmer for a minute.

Serve cauliflower over rice and garnish with scallions and more sesame seeds if desired.

Crispy Tofu Stir Fry

PREP TIME: 15 minutes • **COOK TIME:** 45 minutes • **MAKES:** 4 servings

Easy and delicious this sweet and sour Asian-inspired stir fry is a perfect better-than-takeout dinner!

CRISPY TOFU
1 (16oz) block extra firm tofu
1 teaspoon olive oil
¼ teaspoons salt
⅛ teaspoon pepper
1 ½ tablespoons cornstarch

STIR FRY SAUCE
1 tablespoon sesame oil
¼ cup vegetable broth
3 tablespoons rice vinegar
⅓ cup soy sauce
3 tablespoons maple syrup
1 tablespoon sriracha
2 teaspoons minced ginger
1 ½ tablespoons cornstarch

VEGGIE STIR FRY
1 ½ tablespoons sesame oil
2 tablespoons minced garlic
1 cup sugar snap peas
1 cup carrots, shredded
1 red bell pepper, chopped
¾ cup purple cabbage, sliced
2 cups broccoli, chopped

Preheat oven to 400 degrees F and line a baking sheet with parchment paper. Press tofu to squeeze out as much liquid as possible, then cut into bite-sized cubes. Transfer to a large bowl then drizzle with olive oil. Sprinkle over salt, pepper, and cornstarch and gently toss to coat tofu.

Place onto the baking sheet and bake 30 minutes, flipping halfway.

In a small bowl whisk together the stir fry sauce ingredients. Set aside.

Prepare stir fry by heating sesame oil in a large skillet over medium-high heat. Add minced garlic and sauté 2 minutes. Add peas, carrots, red bell pepper, cabbage and broccoli and cook for 8-10 minutes until crisp and tender, stirring frequently.

Pour in the stir fry sauce and add crispy tofu. Toss so that the tofu and vegetables are coated with the sauce.

Cook an additional 2-3 minutes until heated throughout and the sauce thickens. Serve stir fry over rice or noodles if desired.

One Pot Mushroom Stroganoff

PREP TIME: 2 minutes • **COOK TIME:** 25 minutes • **MAKES:** 4 servings

Packed full of mushrooms in a rich and creamy sauce, this dish is pure comfort! Simple to whip up for a great weeknight meal and sure to satisfy any pasta cravings!

---

3 tablespoons vegan butter
1 ½ cups mushrooms, sliced
½ small white onion, diced
3 teaspoons minced garlic
1 teaspoon thyme
¼ cup flour
3 cups vegetable broth
1 cup almond milk
8 oz rotini noodles, dry
1 teaspoon vegan Worcestershire sauce
1 teaspoon dijon mustard
½ teaspoon salt
¼ teaspoon pepper

Melt the butter in a large pot over medium-high heat. Add mushrooms and onions and cook about 5 minutes, stirring occasionally until the onion is translucent.

Reduce heat to medium then add minced garlic and thyme and cook another 2 minutes.

Sprinkle in flour and cook for about a minute, mixing well, until vegetables are coated evenly and the raw flavor has cooked off the flour.

Pour in vegetable broth and almond milk and add noodles, vegan Worcestershire sauce, and mustard. Mix well, distributing the noodles so they're fully covered by the liquid, then increase heat and bring to a boil.

Boil for 2 minutes, then reduce heat to medium and cook uncovered for 5 minutes. Stir every couple of minutes to ensure even cooking.

Bring the mixture down to a low simmer, then cover and cook an additional 7-10 minutes until pasta is al dente.

Remove from heat then stir in salt and pepper. Taste and adjust seasonings to your liking.

Margherita Pizza

PREP TIME: 10 minutes • **COOK TIME:** 40 minutes • **MAKES:** 1 large pizza

Fresh basil, gooey cashew-based mozzarella, olive oil and garlic on top of a homemade pizza dough - this dish has all the essentials!

PIZZA DOUGH
1 ¾ cup flour
½ teaspoon rapid rise yeast
½ teaspoon sugar
1 cup hot water
2 ½ tablespoons oil (divided)

CASHEW MOZZARELLA
¼ cup raw cashews
½ cup water
1 teaspoon lemon juice
½ teaspoon apple cider vinegar
1 teaspoon white miso
1 tablespoon nutritional yeast
2 ½ tablespoons tapioca starch
¼ teaspoon salt

PIZZA
1 cup marinara sauce
2 teaspoons minced garlic
2 tomatoes, sliced thin
¼ teaspoon seasoned salt
¼ teaspoon red pepper flakes
6 basil leaves, chopped

Preheat oven to 425 degrees F.

In a large bowl whisk together flour, yeast, sugar and salt. Mix in hot water and 1 tbsp olive oil, then knead the dough into a smooth ball. Cover the bowl with plastic wrap and let rest 5 minutes. Meanwhile place cashews in a pot of water over medium heat and bring to a boil.

Roll out the dough on a floured surface to create a circle approximately 14" in diameter. Transfer to a baking sheet and brush the surface of the dough with 1 ½ tbsp olive oil, then bake for 10 minutes.

While the crust is baking, remove cashews from heat and drain. Place in a blender along with fresh water, lemon juice, apple cider vinegar, miso, nutritional yeast, tapioca starch and salt. Blend until very smooth. Pour the watery mixture into a small saucepan over medium heat and stir until it starts to get clumpy, about 2 minutes. Continue stirring just until it binds together in a smooth stretchy ball. Set pan aside.

Remove crust from oven. Mix marinara sauce with minced garlic and spread evenly on top. Add sliced tomato, then drop on dollops of the cashew mozzarella. Return pizza to the oven and bake an additional 17-20 minutes until crust is crisp and lightly browned.

Sprinkle with seasoned salt, red pepper flakes and basil leaves. Slice and enjoy!

Maryland Style Crab-less Cakes

PREP TIME: 1 hour 15 minutes • **COOK TIME:** 10 minutes • **MAKES:** 6 medium patties

These flavor-packed patties give you all of the classic crab cake taste without the guilt. They are amazing alone as well as on a sandwich!

1 (14oz) can hearts of palm
1 cup chickpeas, cooked and drained
20 saltine crackers
2 scallions, chopped
2 tablespoons vegan mayonnaise
½ tablespoon vegan Worcestershire sauce
½ tablespoon dijon mustard
1 tsp dulse flakes
1 tsp parsley
½ teaspoon lemon juice
2 tablespoons Old Bay seasoning
½ teaspoon garlic powder
1 teaspoon vital wheat gluten
1 teaspoon cornstarch

vegetable oil for frying

Dry and finely chop hearts of palm until it closely resembles crab meat, then process or mash chickpeas to flatten.

In a food processor pulse saltine crackers until finely ground. Measure out ¼ cup and set aside.

Add the remaining ground crackers into a shallow bowl, then sprinkle in ½ tablespoon of Old Bay seasoning and mix together to make the breading.

In a large bowl combine all other ingredients including the ¼ cup of reserved ground saltine crackers and remaining Old Bay seasoning, then divide mixture into 6 equal parts and shape each into a round patty.

Dip and swirl each patty into the breading mixture on both sides, then place onto a parchment lined tray and refrigerate for at least an hour to firm.

Heat about 1" of vegetable oil in a frying pan on medium-high heat and cook patties for 4-5 minutes on each side until they are golden brown and cooked through. Place on paper towels to drain excess oil and enjoy warm.

Cauliflower Parmesan Bake

PREP TIME: 5 minutes • **COOK TIME:** 45 minutes • **MAKES:** 4 servings

A vegan take on a classic Italian dish using cauliflower! This recipe will have you craving for more!

1 large head cauliflower
4 tablespoons olive oil
¼ teaspoon salt
⅛ teaspoon pepper
1 cup marinara sauce
½ teaspoon oregano
¼ teaspoon red pepper flakes
2 tablespoons Panko breadcrumbs

CHEESY SAUCE
½ cup cashews
⅓ cup water
½ teaspoon lemon juice
1 teaspoon minced garlic
½ teaspoon onion powder
¼ teaspoon thyme
¼ teaspoon salt

Preheat oven to 425 degrees F and line a baking sheet with parchment paper.

Slice cauliflower vertically into 1" planks and arrange in a single layer on the baking sheet. Brush both sides of each piece with olive oil then season evenly with salt and pepper.

Roast for 20 minutes, then carefully flip cauliflower and roast an additional 20 minutes.

While cauliflower is in the oven prepare cheesy sauce by blending cashews, water, lemon juice, minced garlic, onion powder, thyme and salt until smooth and creamy.

In a small bowl mix together marinara sauce, oregano and red pepper flakes.

Top each cauliflower steak with marinara sauce then the cheesy sauce. Place back into the oven and bake for 5 minutes.

Remove from oven and sprinkle with breadcrumbs. Broil for 30-60 seconds. Watch closely and remove when the top first starts to brown.

Black Bean Lasagna

PREP TIME: 15 minutes • **COOK TIME:** 55 minutes • **MAKES:** 9 servings

Hands down the best lasagna! Macadamia ricotta, black beans, fresh spinach, and topped with an amazing cheesy sauce- it's almost unbelievable this is vegan!

MACADAMIA RICOTTA
- 1 cup macadamia nuts
- 1 teaspoon lemon juice
- ¼ teaspoon salt
- ⅓ cup water

CHEESY SAUCE
- 1 medium carrot, boiled to soften
- ½ cup cashews
- ¼ cup nutritional yeast
- 2 tablespoons vegan butter
- 2 teaspoons vinegar
- ½ teaspoon garlic powder
- ½ teaspoon onion powder
- ¼ teaspoon nutmeg
- ½ teaspoon salt
- ⅛ teaspoon pepper
- ¼ cup vegetable broth
- ⅓ cup water

LASAGNA
- 8 lasagna noodles, cooked
- 1 (25oz) jar pasta sauce
- 2 cups spinach, fresh
- 1 ½ cups black beans, cooked & drained
- 1 teaspoon seasoned salt

Preheat oven to 400 degrees F and grease a 9x13" casserole dish.

Prepare the macadamia ricotta by blending together ricotta ingredients until it's semi-smooth and resembles ricotta. Place mixture into a small bowl.

Next, place the ingredients for the cheesy sauce in a blender and blend until smooth and creamy.

To assemble, layer 4 lasagna noodles to cover the bottom of the dish. Add half of the ricotta mixture and spread evenly over the noodles with the back of a spoon.

Place on one cup of the spinach, then evenly top with half of the jar of pasta sauce. Sprinkle black beans over the dish, crushing with your fingers as you go to flatten most of the beans.

Drizzle with half of the cheesy sauce, then sprinkle ½ teaspoon of seasoned salt on top.

Repeat layer: noodles, macadamia ricotta, spinach, pasta sauce, black beans, cheesy sauce and seasoned salt.

Cover tightly with foil and bake for 55 minutes. Remove from oven and allow to rest at least 30 minutes to firm up for easier slicing.

Desserts

Iced Lemon Loaf Cake

PREP TIME: 10 minutes • **COOK TIME:** 55 minutes • **MAKES:** 1 loaf

Moist, fluffy, tangy and so easy to make from scratch! Every bite of this pound cake is bursting with delicious fresh lemon flavor!

½ cup vegan butter
¾ cup sugar
2 tablespoons applesauce
1 ½ cups flour
½ teaspoon baking powder
¼ teaspoon salt
grated rind from 1 lemon
½ teaspoon lemon juice
¾ cup almond milk

LEMON ICING
¼ cup powdered sugar
1 ¼ tablespoons lemon juice

Preheat oven to 350 degrees F and grease an 8" loaf pan.

In a large bowl add the vegan butter, sugar and applesauce. Cream ingredients together with an electric mixer.

Add in the flour, baking powder, salt, grated lemon rind, lemon juice and almond milk and continue mixing until well combined.

Pour the batter into the loaf pan and bake for 45-55 minutes, until cooked throughout and the top is golden brown. A toothpick should come out clean when inserted into the center of the cake.

Remove from oven and allow cake to cool for 5 minutes.

Meanwhile prepare the icing by whisking together powdered sugar and lemon juice until smooth.

Poke deep holes throughout the top of the loaf with a toothpick, then drizzle the icing on top, as some will flow into the inside of the cake.

Classic Apple Pie

PREP TIME: 10 minutes • **COOK TIME:** 1 hour • **MAKES:** 8 servings

Deliciously crisp and flaky on the outside, soft and sweet on the inside, this fresh apple pie is just like grandma made it!

PIE CRUSTS
- 2 ⅓ cups flour
- 3 tablespoons sugar
- ½ teaspoon salt
- ½ cup vegan butter, cold
- ½ cup vegetable shortening, cold
- 4-6 tablespoons ice cold water

FILLING
- 6 granny smith apples, peeled, cored and diced
- ½ cup vegan butter
- 3 tablespoons flour
- ½ cup sugar
- ⅓ cup brown sugar
- ¼ cup water
- ¾ teaspoon cinnamon

Prepare crust by whisking together flour, sugar and salt in a large bowl. Add the the vegan butter and vegetable shortening and with your hands work the fats into the flour until you have a well combined mixture that is like a coarse meal.

Pour in 4 tablespoons of ice cold water and knead until it starts to clump together. Continue slowly adding water and kneading and pressing just until semi-smooth and holds firmly together.

Divide the dough in half and shape into 2 balls. Dump each ball onto a lightly floured surface and with a rolling pin roll it out to about a 12" circle. Fold one of the circles carefully in half, lift to pie pan, unfold, then press into pan.

Preheat oven to 425 degrees F. Prepare the filling by melting vegan butter in a saucepan. Whisk in flour to form a paste. Mix in sugar, brown sugar and water and bring to a boil. Reduce heat and let simmer about 2 minutes until thickened. Remove from heat.

Fill pie pan with apples, mounded slightly. Gently pour the butter and sugar liquid over the apples, then top with a sprinkle of cinnamon. Cover with the other rolled out pie crust, pressing ends firmly to rim of pan and trimming excess.

Bake for 15 minutes, then reduce temperature to 375 degrees and bake for another 35-45 minutes until apples are soft and crust is golden brown.

Oatmeal Raisin Cookies

PREP TIME: 10 minutes • **COOK TIME:** 17 minutes • **MAKES:** 15-18 cookies

Soft, chewy and thick these delights are loaded with oats and raisins and spiced with cinnamon and nutmeg.

- ¼ cup vegetable shortening
- ¼ cup sugar
- ¼ cup brown sugar
- ¼ applesauce
- ½ teaspoon vanilla extract
- ¼ cup almond milk
- 1 cup flour
- ⅛ teaspoon salt
- ½ teaspoon baking soda
- ¼ teaspoon baking powder
- 1 teaspoon cinnamon
- ½ teaspoon nutmeg
- ½ cup rolled oats
- ½ cup raisins

Preheat oven to 350 degrees F.

In a large bowl cream together vegetable shortening and sugars with an electric mixer. Then add in the applesauce, vanilla extract and almond milk and mix until well combined.

In a separate bowl whisk together flour, salt, baking soda, baking powder, cinnamon and nutmeg.

Add dry mixture to larger bowl along with oats and raisins and mix thoroughly.

Drop by rounded spoonfuls onto a greased or parchment lined baking sheet and bake 15-17 minutes until the tops look just set. Allow to cool fully before removing from baking sheet.

The Best Peanut Butter Cookies

PREP TIME: 5 minutes • **COOK TIME:** 14 minutes • **MAKES:** 8-10 cookies

An easy dessert that's full of peanut butter goodness and made with just a few pantry staples! You're going to love these delightful cookies!

½ cup peanut butter
2 tablespoons applesauce
½ teaspoon vanilla extract
¼ cup flour
¼ cup sugar
¼ teaspoon baking soda
⅛ teaspoon salt

Preheat oven to 350 degrees F and line a baking sheet with parchment paper.

In a small bowl whisk together applesauce and vanilla extract. Set aside.

In a large mixing bowl whisk together the flour, sugar, baking soda and salt.

Add peanut butter and the applesauce mixture to the mixing bowl, then using an electric mixer thoroughly combine all ingredients.

Scoop out heaping teaspoons of dough and roll into balls. Place the balls onto a baking sheet at least 1½" apart, then using a fork make crosshatch lines across the tops of the dough balls, flattening them a bit.

Bake for 12-14 minutes until the edges start to turn a deeper brown.

Let cool for at least 20 minutes before removing from baking sheet. Cookies will initially be very soft but firm up nicely as they cool.

Lemon Blueberry Muffins

PREP TIME: 5 minutes • **COOK TIME:** 25 minutes • **MAKES:** 9 muffins

These muffins are seriously moist, easy to make from scratch and have so much delicious blueberry flavor in every bite with a fresh hint of lemon. You'll never want to make the boxed kind again!

- 1 ½ cups flour
- ¾ cup sugar
- 1 ½ teaspoon baking powder
- ¼ teaspoon baking soda
- ½ teaspoon salt
- ½ cup + 2 tablespoons almond milk
- ⅓ cup vegetable oil
- 1 teaspoon vanilla extract
- 3 tablespoons lemon juice
- 1 ¼ cups blueberries, fresh

Preheat oven to 400 degrees F, then line a muffin pan with 9 paper liners and set aside.

In a large bowl add flour, sugar, baking powder, baking soda and salt and whisk together well.

Slowly stir in the almond milk, then add the vegetable oil, vanilla extract and lemon juice and mix thoroughly.

Add the blueberries to the mixing bowl and carefully fold into the batter, mixing until just combined.

Divide the batter evenly between the 9 muffin cups, filling each just below the top.

Bake for 20-25 minutes until the tops are lightly golden. Remove from the oven when a toothpick inserted into the center of a muffin comes out clean.

1-Hour Cinnamon Rolls

PREP TIME: 30 minutes • **COOK TIME:** 25 minutes • **MAKES:** 9 rolls

Nothing beats hot cinnamon rolls fresh out of the oven and this easy recipe will get you to some deliciously gooey sticky buns pronto!

¾ cup almond milk, hot
¼ cup + 3 teaspoons sugar, divided
1 (¼ oz) packet rapid rise yeast
⅓ cup vegan butter, melted
½ teaspoon salt
2 ½ cups flour
2 tablespoons coconut oil, melted
½ cup brown sugar
3 tablespoons cinnamon

ICING
¾ cup powdered sugar
2 ½ tablespoons almond milk

Pour heated almond milk into a large bowl. Add in 1 teaspoon of sugar and the packet of yeast. Mix well, then let sit for about 10 minutes to activate.

To the bowl add ¼ cup of sugar, melted vegan butter, salt and flour and mix until it forms a soft and slightly sticky dough.

On a lightly floured surface roll out dough into a large rectangle about ¼" thick, then brush surface with melted coconut oil.

Combine brown sugar, cinnamon and 2 teaspoons of sugar into a small bowl, then sprinkle onto dough and smooth evenly with the back of a spoon.

Starting at the long end, roll dough up into a log, then slice off 9 rolls about 1 ½" wide. Place rolls onto greased 9x9 baking pan, cover with plastic wrap and let rest for about 20 minutes to fluff up.

Bake for 25-30 minutes at 350 degrees F until rolls are golden brown.

Prepare icing while rolls are baking by mixing together powdered sugar and almond milk. Drizzle icing on top of the cinnamon rolls once they are out of the oven.

Strawberry Cheesecake Minis

PREP TIME: 20 minutes • **COOK TIME:** 1 hour • **MAKES:** 6 minis

These mini strawberry topped desserts feature a simple 2-ingredient graham cracker crust and a smooth dairy-free cheesecake filling. Easy to make and the perfect portion size!

- 6 whole graham crackers
- 3 tablespoons vegan butter, melted
- 1 cup cashews, raw
- 3 ½ tablespoons coconut oil, melted
- 1 ½ tablespoons lemon juice
- ½ teaspoon vanilla extract
- 4 tablespoons maple syrup
- 2 ripe bananas
- 6 strawberries
- 3 dates, pitted
- 1 teaspoon water

Finely crush graham crackers and mix with melted vegan butter to form the crust. With the back of a spoon press mixture evenly into the bottoms of cupcake molds.

Place cashews, coconut oil, lemon juice, vanilla extract, maple syrup and banana in a blender and process until smooth and creamy. Pour evenly on top of graham cracker base.

In a blender process the strawberries, dates and water until it forms a puree, then spread on top of the filling layer.

Freeze for an hour until filling is firm throughout.

Gently lift cheesecakes out of the molds and enjoy. Store in refrigerator.

Soft Baked Gingersnap Cookies

PREP TIME: 15 minutes • **COOK TIME:** 12 minutes • **MAKES:** 12 cookies

Soft, crinkled molasses cookies spiced with ginger and cinnamon with a crisp edge, they are oozing with amazing-ness in every bite!

- ½ cup flour
- ¼ teaspoon baking soda
- ⅛ teaspoon salt
- ¼ tablespoon ground ginger
- ¼ tablespoon cinnamon
- 3 tablespoons vegetable shortening
- ¼ cup sugar
- 1 tablespoon molasses
- 1 tablespoon applesauce

Preheat oven to 350 degrees F.

Whisk together flour, baking soda, salt, ground ginger and cinnamon in a medium bowl.

In a separate large bowl beat vegetable shortening and sugar with an electric mixer until light and fluffy. Next, add molasses and applesauce and beat until well combined.

Pour in flour mixture and beat until fully mixed.

Shape dough into 1-inch balls and place 2 inches apart on a lined baking sheet.

Bake for 12 minutes. Remove from oven and allow to completely cool on the baking sheet before removing.

Blueberry Twist Bread

PREP TIME: 30 minutes • **COOK TIME:** 40 minutes • **MAKES:** 12 servings

This vegan dessert bread will impress anyone that tastes it! Blueberry preserves are spread onto a soft and fluffy yeast dough, shaped, baked, then drizzled with a sweet vanilla icing. Could it get any better?

¾ cup almond milk, hot
¼ cup + 1 teaspoon sugar
1 (¼ oz) packet rapid rise yeast
⅓ cup vegan butter, melted
1 teaspoon salt
2 ⅓ cups flour
⅔ cup blueberry preserves
1 tablespoon almonds, crushed

VANILLA ICING
½ cup powdered sugar
1 tablespoon almond milk
¼ teaspoon vanilla extract

Pour heated almond milk into a large bowl. Add 1 teaspoon of sugar and yeast. Mix and let sit for 10 minutes to activate.

To the bowl add ¼ cup of sugar, melted vegan butter, salt and flour and mix until it forms a soft and slightly sticky dough.

On floured surface roll out dough into a large rectangle then spread a thin layer of blueberry preserves onto dough evenly with the back of a spoon.

Starting at the long end, tightly roll the dough into a log, then cut the log in half lengthwise. Take the two pieces and carefully wrap them around each other to form a twist, then roll the twist around itself into a circle. Transfer the dough to a 9" springform pan, then cover with plastic wrap and let rest for 10 minutes to fluff up.

Remove plastic then bake for 40 minutes at 375 degrees F until golden brown. Once out of the oven, allow to cool for 10 minutes, then carefully remove from the pan.

In a small bowl whisk together icing ingredients until smooth, then drizzle icing over danish. Sprinkle crushed almonds on top.

Raspberry Almond Thumbprint Cookies

PREP TIME: 1 hour • **COOK TIME:** 18 minutes • **MAKES:** 12-14 cookies

Buttery, crumbly and sweet! Shortbread cookies are taken to the next level with a vibrantly flavored raspberry jam filing and a sweet almond glaze.

1 cup flour
1 teaspoon cornstarch
½ cup vegan butter, softened
¼ cup sugar
¼ teaspoon almond extract
⅓ cup raspberry jam
1 tablespoons water

ALMOND GLAZE
½ cup powdered sugar
¼ teaspoon almond extract
2 teaspoons water

Preheat oven to 350 degrees F.

In a small bowl whisk together the flour and cornstarch. Set aside.

In a large mixing bowl add butter, sugar and ¼ teaspoon of almond extract and with an electric mixer beat on medium speed until creamy.

Reduce speed to low and pour in the flour mixture and combine until well mixed. Cover and refrigerate for one hour.

Pour 1 tablespoon of water into the mixing bowl and combine with the dough.

Shape dough into 1" balls and place on a parchment-lined cookie sheet spaced 2" apart. Make an indentation straight down into the center of each ball with your thumb. Fill each indentation with raspberry jam.

Bake for 14-18 minutes until edges are just slightly browned. Let cookies cool completely.

Combine glaze ingredients in a small bowl and whisk until smooth. Drizzle glaze over cookies.

Double Chocolate Cake w/ Buttercream Frosting

PREP TIME: 15 minutes • **COOK TIME:** 30 minutes • **MAKES:** 10-12 large slices

So rich and full of chocolate goodness this super moist, 2 layer, melt-in-your-mouth cake is the ultimate comfort food!

CHOCOLATE CAKE
- 1 cup almond milk
- 1 tablespoon apple cider vinegar
- 2 cups flour
- 1 ½ cups sugar
- ¾ cup cocoa powder
- 2 teaspoons baking powder
- 1 teaspoon baking soda
- 1 teaspoon salt
- ½ cup vegetable oil
- ½ cup applesauce
- 1 tablespoon vanilla extract
- 1 cup hot water

CHOCOLATE BUTTERCREAM FROSTING
- 3 cups powdered sugar
- ¾ cup cocoa powder
- ¾ cup vegan butter
- 3 ½ tablespoons almond milk
- ½ tablespoon vanilla extract

Preheat oven to 375 degrees F and grease two 9" cake pans.

Pour almond milk and apple cider vinegar into a small bowl and stir. Let sit for 5 minutes.

In a large mixing bowl whisk together the flour, sugar, cocoa powder, baking powder, baking soda and salt.

Next add in the almond milk/apple cider vinegar mixture, vegetable oil, applesauce, vanilla extract and hot water and mix until well combined.

Divide batter evenly between the two cake pans and bake for 30 minutes until cakes are set. Let cool to room temperature before frosting.

Prepare the chocolate buttercream frosting by creaming together the frosting ingredients with an electric mixer until fully combined and smooth.

Stack the cakes one on top of the other, frosting between each layer, around the outside, and on top.

Desserts

Candy Bar Shortbread Cookies

PREP TIME: 15 minutes • **COOK TIME:** 15 minutes • **MAKES:** 12 cookies

Buttery, crisp and utterly delicious shortbread cookies are topped with peanut butter, a chocolate drizzle and crushed peanuts.

- ½ cup vegan butter, softened
- ⅓ cup powdered sugar
- ¾ cup flour
- ¼ teaspoon vanilla extract
- ¼ cup peanut butter
- 4 pieces (1 oz) semi-sweet chocolate bar, melted
- 1 teaspoon almond milk
- 2 tablespoons crushed peanuts

Preheat oven to 325 degrees F.

Add softened vegan butter, powdered sugar, flour and vanilla extract to a large bowl. With an electric mixer, mix together until a crumbly dough forms.

Line the counter with parchment paper and dump the dough onto the counter. Knead and press the dough into a ball. Place another piece of parchment paper on top of the dough ball and roll out flat to about a ¼" thickness.

Using a cookie cutter cut into approximately 2 ½" diameter circles and carefully transfer each onto a parchment lined baking sheet. Bake for about 15 minutes until the bottoms of the cookies just begin to brown. Remove from the oven and allow to cool completely.

Evenly spread peanut butter on tops of cookies. Whisk together melted chocolate and almond milk then drizzle on top of peanut butter. Finish with a sprinkle of crushed peanuts.

Chewy Snickerdoodle Cookies

PREP TIME: 10 minutes • **COOK TIME:** 10 minutes • **MAKES:** 28-30 cookies

Soft, buttery delights covered in cinnamon and sugar with a signature tang from cream of tartar! These are pure cozy comfort in cookie form!

2 ½ cups flour
1 teaspoon cream of tartar
½ teaspoon baking soda
⅛ teaspoon salt
1 cup vegan butter
¾ cup sugar
¼ cup applesauce
1 ½ teaspoon vanilla extract

TOPPING
2 ½ tablespoons sugar
1 tablespoon cinnamon

Preheat oven to 375 degrees F.

In a large bowl whisk together the flour, cream of tartar, baking soda and salt. Set aside.

In a separate large mixing bowl cream butter and sugar until light and fluffy using an electric mixer. Scrape the sides of the bowl then add applesauce and vanilla extract. Cream 1-2 minutes longer.

Add in the flour mixture and combine until flour is fully incorporated.

To make the topping: in a small bowl stir together the sugar and cinnamon.

Taking about 2 tablespoons of dough at a time, shape into balls, then roll the balls in the cinnamon-sugar mixture until evenly coated.

Place balls on a parchment-lined baking sheet, spaced about 2" apart.

Bake for 9 minutes. The cookies will initially be very soft. Let cool at least 10 minutes on the baking sheet before removing.

Acknowledgements

I want to take a moment to express my heartfelt gratitude to everyone who helped make this book happen.

To my subscribers, followers, and virtual friends I have gained over the years - THANK YOU. Thank you for your encouragement and support. Thank you for trusting me and growing with me. To have an audience that has made me feel comfortable enough to share my interests and talents on such a large scale means everything. Thank you for seeing something in me and igniting the spark that gave me the idea to even create this book. You guys have been so instrumental in helping me unlock my creativity. This one's for all of you.

To my carnivore friends, thanks for always thinking of me and making sure I have plenty to eat at group gatherings and to being open to trying plant-based foods. You guys rock.

A huge thank you to my family for being my willing in-house taste testers. You always tell me like it is and have truly shaped this book to be a perfect reflection of vegan cuisine that is appealing to all. I hope it wasn't too annoying maneuvering around all the foodstuff I always had out in the kitchen in the making of this book.

Thanks to the countless people who have given me ideas and recipe suggestions. I have tried to incorporate as many as possible and hope these tantalize your taste buds and impress everyone you share a bite with. Enjoy!

Conversion Charts

TEMPERATURE

FAHRENHEIT	CELSIUS
250°F	120°C
275°F	135°C
300°F	150°C
325°F	160°C
350°F	180°C
375°F	190°C
400°F	200°C
425°F	220°C
450°F	230°C

WEIGHT

U.S. / IMPERIAL	METRIC
1/2 oz	15 g
1 oz	30 g
2 oz	60 g
1/4 lb	115 g
1/3 lb	150 g
1/2 lb	225 g
3/4 lb	350 g
1 lb	450 g

VOLUME

U.S.	IMPERIAL	METRIC
1 tablespoon	1/2 fl oz	15 ml
2 tablespoons	1 fl oz	30 ml
1/4 cup	2 fl oz	60 ml
1/3 cup	3 fl oz	90 ml
1/2 cup	4 fl oz	120 ml
2/3 cup	5 fl oz	150 ml
3/4 cup	6 fl oz	180 ml
1 cup	8 fl oz	240 ml
2 cups	16 fl oz	480 ml

Copyright © 2020 by TheChicNatural

All Rights Reserved. No part of this book may be reproduced in any form or by any electronic or mechanical means, including information storage and retrieval systems, without permission in writing from the author.

Published in the United States.

Photographs © 2020 by TheChicNatural

Hardcover ISBN: 978-1-7354825-0-7

First Edition